"This is maybe the best short theology of M(is how he places Mark in conversation with composed his work, Peter and Paul were al Gospel. Mark more fully narrates the story of this great hero who is more than the Jewish Messiah. He is the divine Son."

> **Patrick Schreiner,** Associate Professor of New Testament and Biblical Theology, Midwestern Baptist Theological Seminary; author, *The Kingdom of God and the Glory of the Cross* and *The Visual Word*

"Peter Orr offers readers a rich biblical-theological treatment of the Gospel of Mark, which summons us to follow Christ, the Son of God and servant King. Orr insightfully calls Mark 'the beginning of the gospel,' drawing historical and theological links between this foundational narrative of Jesus's life and the apostolic preaching of Paul and Peter. This is essential reading for all who study and teach Mark's Gospel."

> **Brian J. Tabb,** Academic Dean and Professor of Biblical Studies, Bethlehem College & Seminary

"Peter Orr offers a brief, accessible, and insightful survey of the theology of Mark's Gospel. Orr emphasizes in *The Beginning of the Gospel* what Mark emphasizes—the gospel of Jesus Christ—and invites readers to see connections between this Gospel and the epistles of the apostle Paul. This book will equip both specialists and general readers to read and reread Mark's Gospel with deeper understanding and appreciation."

> **Guy Prentiss Waters,** James M. Baird, Jr. Professor of New Testament and Academic Dean, Reformed Theological Seminary, Jackson

The Beginning of the Gospel

New Testament Theology

Edited by Thomas R. Schreiner and Brian S. Rosner

The Beginning of the Gospel: A Theology of Mark, Peter Orr

From the Manger to the Throne: A Theology of Luke, Benjamin L. Gladd

The Mission of the Triune God: A Theology of Acts, Patrick Schreiner

United to Christ, Walking in the Spirit: A Theology of Ephesians, Benjamin L. Merkle

The God Who Judges and Saves: A Theology of 2 Peter and Jude, Matthew S. Harmon

The Joy of Hearing: A Theology of the Book of Revelation, Thomas R. Schreiner

The Beginning of the Gospel

A Theology of Mark

Peter Orr

:: CROSSWAY®

WHEATON, ILLINOIS

For Ben, Ollie, Jonny, and Daniel

Contents

Series Preface

THERE ARE REMARKABLY FEW TREATMENTS of the big ideas of single books of the New Testament. Readers can find brief coverage in Bible dictionaries, in some commentaries, and in New Testament theologies, but such books are filled with other information and are not devoted to unpacking the theology of each New Testament book in its own right. Technical works concentrating on various themes of New Testament theology often have a narrow focus, treating some aspect of the teaching of, say, Matthew or Hebrews in isolation from the rest of the book's theology.

The New Testament Theology series seeks to fill this gap by providing students of Scripture with readable book-length treatments of the distinctive teaching of each New Testament book or collection of books. The volumes approach the text from the perspective of biblical theology. They pay due attention to the historical and literary dimensions of the text, but their main focus is on presenting the teaching of particular New Testament books about God and his relations to the world on their own terms, maintaining sight of the Bible's overarching narrative and Christocentric focus. Such biblical theology is of fundamental importance to biblical and expository preaching and informs exegesis, systematic theology, and Christian ethics.

The twenty volumes in the series supply comprehensive, scholarly, and accessible treatments of theological themes from an evangelical perspective. We envision them being of value to students, preachers, and interested laypeople. When preparing an expository sermon series, for example, pastors can find a healthy supply of informative commentaries, but there are few options for coming to terms with the overall teaching of each book of the New Testament. As well as being useful in sermon and Bible study preparation, the volumes will also be of value as textbooks in college and seminary exegesis classes. Our prayer is that they contribute to a deeper understanding of and commitment to the kingdom and glory of God in Christ.

Peter Orr's Mark volume, *The Beginning of the Gospel,* demonstrates that underlying Mark's concise and energetic historical account of Jesus lies profound theology connected to every part of Scripture, especially the Old Testament and the writings of Paul and Peter. If Peter is Mark's historical source, Paul is Mark's theological partner. According to Orr, Mark provides "the beginning of the gospel," forging historical and theological connections between Jesus's life and ministry and the preaching of the apostles. Mark's Gospel calls us to follow Jesus, the divine Son and servant King, who inaugurates the long-awaited kingdom of God and whose death is a model for us to emulate and a ransom for our sins.

Thomas R. Schreiner and Brian S. Rosner

Preface

THIS BOOK IS MY ATTEMPT TO CAPTURE some of the main themes of Mark's Gospel. As the shortest and earliest Gospel, Mark gives us a crisp, fast-paced picture of Jesus. However, I discovered (although it should have been obvious) that Mark does not *simply* write a stand-alone piece. Not only does he draw from the rich resources of the Old Testament, but he also consciously writes with an awareness of other New Testament voices (particularly Paul and Peter). As the first Gospel to be written, Mark is something of a linchpin for the New Testament, in fact for the whole Bible, as voices from the Old Testament and the New Testament join in a conversation that centers on the most important person in history. I hope this book helps you to become more excited about Mark and, more importantly, about Jesus.

I am very thankful to many people for their help and support during the writing of this book. First and foremost, my sincere thanks to the governing board of Moore Theological College for granting me six months of study leave to work on this volume. Thank you to my friend, colleague, and the principal of the college, Mark Thompson, for his encouragement to use my study leave in this way.

Thank you to Tom Schreiner and Brian Rosner for inviting me to contribute to this series and for their encouragement as I have written this book. Thank you to everyone at Crossway, especially to Chris Cowan whose editorial skill has greatly improved this volume.

My colleagues on the faculty at Moore College have been a wonderful support during this project in different ways. I want to especially thank my friends and colleagues in the New Testament department—Chris Conyers, Philip Kern, Will Timmins, and Lionel Windsor. Philip, in addition to being a great friend, colleague, and department head, is a wonderful model of godly, careful teaching. It has been a delight to sit and listen to him lecture in the classes we teach together. Thanks as well to Simon Gillham, Chase Kuhn, and Paul Grimmond for their friendship and frequent encouragement.

A number of people have very kindly read portions of this book or helped with its production in other ways. Thank you to Jeff Aernie, Joel Atwood, Keith Hill, and Adam Wood. Philip Kern gave detailed feedback for which I am especially grateful.

Thanks to the wonderful church family at All Saints Petersham. I also want to acknowledge a number of friends who have, in different ways, given encouragement or support during this writing process and for whom I am very thankful to God: Ben and Sara Gray, Russ and Aimee Grinter, Luke and Anna Jackson, Paul and Caroline Ritchie, and Ross and Megan Walker.

Writing this during the COVID-19 pandemic and with borders closed, I have more than ever felt the distance from my parents Philip and Kay and my sister Susannah in the UK. I hope we can see each other soon. I am very grateful to you, Em, as always and for everything.

Finally, to the dedicatees of this book, my four sons—the arrows in my quiver/liver—I love you all and hope that you will always believe in, follow, and love the Jesus of Mark's Gospel (now get off your devices and tidy your rooms).

Soli Deo Gloria!
Peter Orr
Sydney, 2021

Abbreviations

AB	Anchor Bible
ATJ	*Ashland Theological Journal*
BBR	*Bulletin for Biblical Research*
BDAG	Bauer, Walter, Frederick W. Danker, William F. Arndt, and F. Wilbur Gingrich. *Greek-English Lexicon of the New Testament and Other Early Christian Literature.* 3rd ed. Chicago: University of Chicago Press, 2000
BECNT	Baker Exegetical Commentary on the New Testament
BIS	Biblical Interpretation Series
BNTC	Black's New Testament Commentary
BZNW	Beihefte zur Zeitschrift für die neutestamentliche Wissenschaft
CBQ	*Catholic Biblical Quarterly*
JBL	*Journal of Biblical Literature*
JSNT	*Journal for the Study of the New Testament*
LCL	Loeb Classical Library
LNTS	Library of New Testament Studies
LXX	Septuagint
MT	Masoretic Text
NETS	News English Translation of the Septuagint
NIGTC	New International Greek Testament Commentary
NSBT	New Studies in Biblical Theology

NTL	New Testament Library
NTS	*New Testament Studies*
PNTC	Pillar New Testament Commentaries
RTR	*Reformed Theological Review*
SBLDS	Society of Biblical Literature Dissertation Series
SNTSMS	Society for New Testament Studies Monograph Series
TNTC	Tyndale New Testament Commentaries
TynBul	*Tyndale Bulletin*
WBC	Word Biblical Commentary
WUNT	Wissenschaftliche Untersuchungen zum Neuen Testament
ZECNT	Zondervan Exegetical Commentary on the New Testament
ZNW	*Zeitschrift für die neutestamentliche Wissenschaft*

Introduction

The Beginning of the Gospel

Mark as Backstory

MARK STARTS AT THE BEGINNING. His first words are "the beginning [*archē*] of the gospel." This phrase, lacking a verb as it does, functions as the title for the book.[1] Mark has written the beginning, origin, or backstory of the gospel that has been preached about Jesus.[2]

A first-century Christian who read Mark would have understood the "gospel" as a message to be heard, not a book to be read. That is the way Mark uses the term *gospel* (*euangelion*) throughout his work (1:14, 15; 8:35; 10:29; 13:10; 14:9)—always a message that is preached and heard. After Mark wrote, his book became known as a "Gospel," thus creating two related but distinct understandings of the word *gospel* (i.e., a book about Jesus's life or a message about him that is preached). However, as Mark writes, the gospel was only known as a preached message. Mark, then, is providing his readers with the beginning—that is, the fleshed out, detailed backstory to the gospel they had heard preached.

---

1 For a detailed defense of this position see M. Eugene Boring, "Mark 1:1–15 and the Beginning of the Gospel," *Semeia* 52 (1991): 43–81.

2 I am assuming the traditional argument that the author of this Gospel is John Mark (mentioned in, e.g., Acts 12:12; 15:39). For a good survey of the issues, see Eckhard J. Schnabel, *Mark: An Introduction and Commentary*, TNTC (Downers Grove, IL: IVP Academic, 2017), 7–12.

Thinking about this book as the backstory to the gospel invites us to consider Mark in relation to the two (for want of a better word) *leading* apostles in the New Testament: Peter and Paul. Put simply, Peter is Mark's historical source while Paul is his theological conversation partner.

Peter: Mark's Historical Source

Traditionally, Mark has been associated with the apostle Peter, while Luke has been associated with Paul. In Eusebius's *Ecclesiastical History*, he discusses "the extant five books of Papias" (a second-century bishop of Hierapolis).[3] At one point he quotes what Papias says about Mark: "Mark, having become the interpreter of Peter, wrote down accurately, though not in order, whatsoever he remembered of the things said or done by Christ."[4] This quote is subject to considerable debate, but we need simply to note the clear, early association made between Mark and Peter.

A little later, Irenaeus, bishop of Lyons, also wrote about how the Gospels came to be written. He records that "Mark, the disciple and interpreter of Peter, did also hand down to us in writing what had been preached by Peter. Luke also, the companion of Paul, recorded in a book the Gospel preached by him."[5] Here again, we have Mark described as the "interpreter of Peter," while Luke is associated with Paul.

There are also indications in Mark's Gospel itself that point to Peter's influence. An inclusio in the narrative has Peter as the first (1:16) and last (16:7) named disciple.[6] Richard Bauckham suggests that this may be an ancient literary device to indicate Peter as the eyewitness on

---

3   Eusebius, *Ecclesiastical History, Books 1–5*, trans. Kirsopp Lake, LCL (Cambridge, MA: Harvard University Press, 1926), 3.39.1.

4   Eusebius, *Ecclesiastical History* 3.39.15.

5   Irenaeus, *Against Heresies* 3.1.1., in *The Apostolic Fathers, Justin Martyr, Irenaeus*; vol. 1 in *Ante-Nicene Fathers*, ed. Alexander Roberts, James Donaldson, and A. Cleveland Coxe, trans. Alexander Roberts and William Rambaut (Buffalo, NY: Christian Literature, 1885), http://www.newadvent.org, rev. and ed. Kevin Knight for New Advent.

6   Richard Bauckham, *Jesus and the Eyewitnesses: The Gospels as Eyewitness Testimony*, 2nd ed. (Grand Rapids, MI: Eerdmans, 2017), 124–25.

whose testimony the narrative depends.[7] Other details highlight Peter as well—such as the double reference to Simon Peter in 1:16 (Jesus saw "*Simon* and Andrew the brother of *Simon*") and the inclusion of Peter's name in 16:7 ("go, tell his disciples *and Peter*").[8]

Peter is certainly the most prominent disciple in the Gospel, mentioned by Mark more frequently (proportionally) than by Matthew or Luke. At points in the narrative Peter is the disciple who is the focus, perhaps most notably in his dialogue with Jesus in 8:31–38 (cf. 9:5; 10:28; 11:21; 14:29, 37, 54–72).[9] Furthermore, while Mark frequently "narrates what different characters see and hear . . . the act of remembering is only attributed to Peter."[10] In 11:21 Peter remembers the fig tree Jesus cursed, and in 14:72 he remembers Jesus's prediction of his denial. These and other features that highlight Peter's perspective suggest that Mark is telling his Gospel primarily through the lens and perspective of Peter.[11]

One potential objection to this view is that Mark often portrays Peter in a negative light. However, we will see that the portrayal of Peter is complex and certainly not wholly negative. In any case, the first readers of Mark would know that Peter ultimately underwent a transformation, and the Gospel itself indicates that this would happen (e.g., 16:7).

None of these features provides incontrovertible proof of Petrine influence on Mark's Gospel, but together with the testimony of Papias and Irenaeus they point to a likely link between Peter and Mark's Gospel. Mark, it seems, has written his Gospel from Peter's perspective.

7   Bauckham, *Jesus and the Eyewitnesses*, 132–45.

8   Michael Bird, "Mark: Interpreter of Peter and Disciple of Paul," in *Paul and the Gospels: Christologies, Conflicts and Convergences,* ed. Michael F. Bird and Joel Willits, LNTS 411 (London: T&T Clark, 2011), 35.

9   Bauckham, *Jesus and the Eyewitnesses*, 126.

10   Finn Damgaard, "Persecution and Denial—Paradigmatic Apostolic Portrayals in Paul and Mark," in *Mark and Paul: Comparative Essays Part II: For and Against Pauline Influence on Mark*, ed. Eve-Marie Becker, Troels Engberg-Pedersen, and Mogens Müller, BZNW 199 (Berlin: De Gruyter, 2014), 297.

11   Bauckham, *Jesus and the Eyewitnesses*, 155–82.

Paul: Mark's Theological Partner

This close connection between Mark and Peter meant that any possible relationship between Mark and Paul was left largely unexplored until the nineteenth century with the publication of two monographs by the German scholar Gustav Volkmar.[12] Volkmar argued that Mark's Gospel was essentially an allegorical defense of Paul. He suggested that Jesus in Mark represents Paul, Jesus's family stands for the Jerusalem church led by James, and the Pharisees correspond to Paul's opponents. Volkmar's argument was largely refuted by Martin Werner in a 1923 monograph.[13] As a result, although the relationship between Paul and Mark was periodically touched on in scholarship, it was not until the publication of an article by Joel Marcus in 2000 that scholarly focus turned to the question.[14] Marcus's article has sparked a mini-revival in the study of Mark's dependence on Paul, and if we can speak of a scholarly consensus, it seems to be now held that Mark wrote under the theological influence of Paul.

One of the clearest connections between Paul and Mark is their use of the word "gospel" (*euangelion*). The word "gospel" occurs four times in Matthew (Matt. 4:23; 9:35; 24:14; 26:13), twice in Acts (Acts 15:7; 20:24), and not at all in Luke or John.[15] Its appearance seven times[16] in Mark makes it the New Testament book with the most occurrences outside of Paul (the only two other occurrences are in 1 Pet. 4:17 and Rev. 14:6). In the New Testament, this is a particularly Pauline and Markan word. Even the phrase with which Mark starts his work, "the beginning of the gospel," is found in

---

12 Gustav Volkmar, *Die Religion Jesu* (Leipzig: Brockhaus, 1857); Gustav Volkmar, *Die Evangelien oder Marcus und die Synopse der kanonischen und ausserkanonischen Evangelien nach dem ältesten Text mit historisch-exegetischem Commentar* (Leipzig: Fuess, 1870).

13 Martin Werner, *Der Einfluss paulinischer Theologie im Markusevangelium: eine Studie zur neutestamentlichen Theologie*, BZNW 1 (Giessen: Töpelmann, 1923).

14 Joel Marcus, "Mark—Interpreter of Paul," *NTS* 46 (2000): 473–87.

15 Luke does frequently use the verb *euangelizō*.

16 It also appears an eighth time in Mark 16:15, but I have omitted this since 16:9–20 is likely not original.

Paul when he reminds the Philippian church of their partnership with him "in the beginning of the gospel" (*en archē tou euangeliou*; Phil. 4:15).[17]

The strong parallels are found not only in the frequency of usage but also in the ways in which Mark and Paul employ the word *gospel*. Paul tends to refer to "the gospel" without modifiers (e.g., Rom. 1:16; 10:16; 1 Cor. 4:15).[18] Apart from 1:1 and 1:14, Mark also writes the word without any modifiers, as opposed to Matthew who tends to use modifiers (e.g., "the gospel of the kingdom" in 4:23; 9:35; 24:14).

For Paul, the gospel can be an "episodic narrative"[19] expressed in two stages as seen in 1 Thessalonians 4:14: "we believe that [1] Jesus died and [2] rose again." Or it can be expressed in multiple episodes as in 1 Corinthians 15:3–8: "[1] Christ died . . . [2] was buried . . . [3] was raised . . . [4] appeared." It seems that part of Mark's reason for writing is to "render the Pauline oral gospel episodic narrative for the first time into a written long-form episodic narrative."[20]

Paul and Mark share a number of additional theological convictions. I will touch on these in later chapters, but at this stage I can note the following: the inability for people to naturally understand the cross (cf. Mark 8:31–33 and 1 Cor. 1:18); the attitude to the law, particularly concerning food (cf. Mark 7:18–19 and Rom. 14:20); the temporal priority of mission to Israel and then to the world (cf. Mark 7:26–27 and Rom. 1:16); the relationship between Jesus and Rome (cf. Mark 12:17 and Rom. 13:1).[21]

---

17 Paul here is referring to the beginning of the Philippians' association with the gospel. So G. Walter Hansen, *The Letter to the Philippians*, PNTC (Grand Rapids, MI: Eerdmans, 2009), 318.

18 Willi Marxsen, *Mark the Evangelist: Studies on the Redaction History of the Gospel*, trans. James Boyce, Donald Juel, William Poehlmann, and Roy A. Harrisville (Nashville: Abingdon, 1969), 127.

19 Margaret Mitchell, "Mark, the Long-Form Pauline εὐαγγέλιον," in *Modern and Ancient Literary Criticism of the Gospels: Continuing the Debate on Gospel Genre(s)*, ed. R. M. Calhoun, D. P. Moessner, and T. Nicklas, WUNT 451 (Tübingen: Mohr Siebeck, 2020), 211.

20 Mitchell, "Mark, the Long-Form Pauline εὐαγγέλιον," 211.

21 For more see Mar Pérez i Díaz, *Mark, A Pauline Theologian*, WUNT 2.521 (Tübingen: Mohr Siebeck, 2020), 45–190.

For Marcus, however, their shared understanding of the cross is their clearest point of similarity. For both Mark and Paul, the death of Jesus, in addition to bringing salvation, is an "apocalyptic event"—that is, one that reveals what could not otherwise be known.[22] Paul speaks of the cross in apocalyptic terms in 1 Corinthians 1–2 (e.g., the cross being the "secret and hidden wisdom of God" in 1 Cor. 2:7). As Mark narrates the crucifixion, he highlights the apocalyptic phenomena that occurred around Jesus's death (particularly the darkness of 15:33 and the torn curtain of 15:38). His narrative climaxes with a moment of "apocalyptic revelation" when the centurion grasps his identity as the Son of God—precisely at the moment of his death (15:39).[23]

These parallels between Mark and Paul are significant. As Marcus puts it, "The other Gospels do not concentrate on the cross as single-mindedly as Mark does. Nor do they share to the same extent the Markan emphasis that this apocalyptic demonstration of divine power took place in an arena of stark human weakness."[24] He notes that Mark is the only Gospel that narrates the first human confession of Jesus's sonship as occurring at the cross.[25]

There may be a particular connection between Mark's Gospel and Paul's letter to the Romans. Scholars (inevitably!) debate the location from which Mark wrote his Gospel, but a good case can be made that he wrote from Rome.[26] For example, it has been noted that ten of the eighteen Latinisms in the New Testament (i.e., Greek transliterations of Latin loanwords) are found in Mark's Gospel (e.g., *dēnarion* in 6:37; 12:15; 14:5; *praitōrion* in 15:16). This is "a frequency which is higher than any other Greek literary text of the period."[27] The "most likely

---

22 Marcus, "Mark—Interpreter of Paul," 479.
23 Marcus, "Mark—Interpreter of Paul," 480.
24 Marcus, "Mark—Interpreter of Paul," 482.
25 Marcus, "Mark—Interpreter of Paul," 483. Cf. Matt. 16:16; Luke 1:32, 35; John 1:49.
26 See Brian J. Incigneri, *The Gospel to the Romans: The Setting and Rhetoric of Mark's Gospel*, BIS (Leiden: Brill, 2003), for a more comprehensive defense of this position.
27 Michael P. Theophilus, "The Roman Connection: Paul and Mark," in *Paul and Mark: Comparative Essays Part I: Two Authors at the Beginnings of Christianity*, ed. Oda Wisch-meyer, David C. Sim, and Ian J. Elmer, BZNW 198 (Berlin: De Gruyter, 2014), 50.

place for Latinisms to predominate is in the city of Rome, where the Latin and Greek languages were closely intermingled as nowhere else at the time."[28]

If Mark did write from Rome (and I am only raising it as a possibility), it is interesting to note that the two descriptions of the "gospel" at the beginning of Romans ("the gospel of his Son" in Rom. 1:9; "the gospel of God" in Rom. 1:1) match those at the beginning of Mark ("the gospel of Jesus Christ, the Son of God" in Mark 1:1; "the gospel of God" in Mark 1:14).

Mark has strong parallels in theological emphases with Paul, particularly his letter to the Romans. That is not to say that there aren't parallels with other New Testament writers. However, the shared theological emphases between Mark and Paul suggest a closer affinity between the two writers.

Reading Mark with Peter and Paul: Mark as Backstory

Michael Bird has helpfully shown that lining up Mark's Gospel with *either* Peter *or* Paul is reductionistic. In fact, the New Testament associates Mark with *both* Peter (1 Pet. 5:13) *and* Paul (e.g., Acts 12:25; Col. 4:10; 2 Tim. 4:11; Philem. 1:24). He suggests that the Gospel of Mark reflects the influence of both and is best thought of as "Petrine testimony shaped into an evangelical narrative conducive to Pauline proclamation."[29]

How does this help us read Mark's Gospel? In the first place it reminds us that Mark is writing both history *and* theology. He is writing a historical account of what Jesus said and did. Though not an eyewitness himself,[30] Mark writes his account in conversation with one of the main eyewitnesses who was with Jesus for almost the duration of the events that are described. At the same time, Mark is not simply writing "pure history," if such a thing even exists. Comparing

28 Incigneri, *The Gospel to the Romans*, 102.

29 Bird, "Mark: Interpreter of Peter and Disciple of Paul," 32.

30 The suggestion that the young man in 14:51–52 who flees naked is a reference to Mark is intriguing but unlikely.

Mark to the other Gospels shows that he has made choices concerning the order of his narrative and what he includes and omits. These choices are made for theological reasons. When, for example, we read of people's repeated inability to grasp the truth about Jesus, Mark is showing us the theological point that without Jesus opening people's eyes (as he does so dramatically in 8:22–26), they cannot grasp the truth of who he is.

This book traces some of the main theological themes in Mark's Gospel. Consequently, the connection with Paul in particular will help us as we read the Gospel. Although the Gospels come first in our New Testament (because they describe the earliest events in the period), it is helpful to remember that Paul's letters were the first widely circulated Christian writings (with 1 Thessalonians probably the first written).[31] And so, while Mark and Paul both write about the gospel, they do so from different perspectives. Paul unfolds the significance of the gospel for the churches that he writes to, while Mark gives the beginning—the backstory—of the gospel as it is found in the life and teaching of Jesus.

Mark is writing in the context of an already known and understood gospel, particularly in the form in which it was preached by Paul. Therefore, although we can and should read Mark on his own terms, by titling his work as "the beginning of the gospel," he is deliberately inviting people to read it in conversation with the already known and preached gospel. This is not an argument that Mark necessarily writes with a copy of Paul's letter to the Romans in front of him (although this is not impossible) but that he is writing in conversation with (particularly) the form of Pauline Christianity that we see expressed in Paul's letters.

There are a number of implications that flow from this relationship between Mark and Paul. First, we should not expect that every concept that Mark introduces will receive the fullest explanation. We see this even with his reference to the gospel. As I noted, it is introduced in the

---

31 The Gospel writings themselves may draw on early written sources, but these do not seem to have been widely circulated (such that they only survive in the form in which they are found in the Gospels).

first verse and referenced six other times in the book (1:14, 15; 8:35; 10:29; 13:10; 14:9), but it is nowhere defined. Mark assumes that his readers will have an understanding of the content of the gospel (the preached message about Jesus) and offers a basic commentary on that gospel message. Twice he refers to the widespread proclamation of the gospel ("all nations" in 13:10; "the whole world" in 14:9). Mark writes in a context where this has already begun to happen.

Second, Mark's Gospel was written for Christians. This does *not* mean that a non-Christian could not read it and come to understand the gospel. Mark's Gospel obviously includes enough to bring a non-believer to faith (as no doubt has happened throughout history). However, this does not negate the fact that Mark wrote for Christians with an awareness of the basic gospel message. We see a parallel in Luke's Gospel, which was written to give a Christian (whether Theophilus is a real or stylized person) "certainty concerning the things" that he had been taught (Luke 1:4).

Third, understanding Mark to be writing in self-conscious conversation with Paul will help us at different points of interpretation. One of the challenges in reading the narrative sections of the Bible is that sometimes it can be hard to know why a writer has included a particular account. What theological point is he making? Reading Mark in conversation with Paul (in particular) gives us a control, in that often the theological point being made will have a parallel in Paul.

Fourth, this reading of Mark helps us in the other direction also— as we read Paul's letters. We can see the theological points that Paul makes grounded and narrated in the life of Jesus. This does not merely establish their truthfulness (showing that Paul is faithfully discharging his role as an apostle of Christ); it also allows us to see his theological points demonstrated and lived out. For instance, in 1 Corinthians 2:14 Paul writes, "The natural person does not accept the things of the Spirit of God, for they are folly to him, and he is not able to understand them because they are spiritually discerned." We see this reality played out across the narrative of Mark's Gospel as people consistently fail to grasp the truth about Jesus.

Thinking of Mark as the backstory to the gospel finds an imperfect parallel in the writings of C. S. Lewis. I say "imperfect" because analogies like this can easily take on a life of their own! However, it may help to think of the relationship between Mark and Romans as *somewhat* similar to the relationship between *The Magician's Nephew* and the more famous *The Lion, the Witch and the Wardrobe*.[32] This more well-known volume was written first. *The Magician's Nephew* was written five years later (with three books in between) but narrates events that occurred before the story contained in *The Lion, the Witch and the Wardrobe*. The books each stand alone as wonderful works of fiction, but readers who have read both have a richer, fuller, and more complete understanding of the overall story arc.[33]

Mark writes to narrate "the beginning of the gospel"—to give the backstory to the proclamation of the message about Jesus. The title also anticipates the end of the book. Famously, the book finishes with the women fleeing from the empty tomb in amazement and not saying anything to anyone "for they were afraid" (16:8).[34] The risen Christ does not appear, and the Gospel seems to end in an anticlimactic way. However, the identity of this volume as "the beginning of the gospel" fits with the abruptness of the ending. Mark writes in a context where the gospel is known and where people *have* communicated the gospel, unlike the women who fled because of fear. He also writes with an implied encouragement that his readers will continue to be involved in the proclamation of the gospel. The abrupt ending reflects the fact that "Mark's Gospel is just the *beginning* of the good news, because Jesus's story has become ours, and we take it up where Mark leaves off."[35]

---

32 C. S. Lewis, *The Lion, the Witch and the Wardrobe* (London: Geoffrey Bles, 1950); C. S. Lewis, *The Magician's Nephew* (London: Bodley Head, 1955).

33 I refuse to enter into the highly charged debate about the proper reading order of the Narnia series!

34 The Greek is even more abrupt, with the last word being the word "for" (*gar*). Because of this abruptness, a number of longer endings can be found in some manuscripts, but it seems unlikely that any of these are original.

35 Joel Marcus, *Mark 8–16: A New Translation with Introduction and Commentary*, AB (New Haven, CT: Yale University Press, 2009), 1096.

It is right to approach Mark's Gospel as a coherent and stand-alone account of Jesus's life. It can be read wholly and meaningfully on its own terms. This present volume will not simply be a study of Mark in conversation with Paul. I will also concentrate on what Mark himself says about the different themes we consider. However, Mark's Gospel, as the first Gospel to be written, invites us to read it in conversation with the rest of the New Testament (and, as we will see, the Old Testament), as it narrates for us "the *beginning* of the gospel."

Divine Identity

Jesus Christ, the Son of God

EVEN THOUGH MARK WRITES a book to explain the origins of the gospel, his central focus is on Jesus since the gospel is *about* Jesus.[1] Therefore, this book on Mark will really be a book about Jesus! I will more narrowly concentrate in this chapter on two aspects of Jesus's identity: (1) the titles used of him and (2) how his miracles reveal his divine identity. There will be overlap between the sections since some of the titles indicate his divine identity. There is, however, more to say about Jesus because Mark says much about what Jesus does. So although this chapter focuses on Jesus, the remainder of the book will build on our understanding of who he is.

The Titles of Jesus

In this section, then, I will examine the titles of Jesus. Whole monographs have been written on each of these titles; thus, all I can do here is sketch the main contours that each brings to Mark's picture of Jesus.

---

1 One can understand the Greek expression *euangelion Iēsou Christou* in 1:1 as a subjective genitive—that is, "the gospel preached by Jesus Christ." We do read of Jesus proclaiming the "gospel of God" in 1:14. However, as I have argued above, the titular nature of 1:1 fits better with the idea that this book describes the beginning of the gospel *about* Jesus, rather than the gospel that Jesus preached.

In a book that starts by identifying its main character as the "Christ" and "the Son of God" (Mark 1:1),[2] that pivots on Peter confessing Jesus as the Christ (8:29), and that climaxes (to a degree) with the confession of the Roman centurion that Jesus was the "Son of God" (15:39), the titles used of Jesus are clearly significant. Certainly, Mark's view of Jesus cannot be reduced to a study of the titles, but to neglect them would be to overlook a rich seam of information about the person of Jesus.

Christ

Although "Christ" (*Christos* in Greek; *Messiah* in Hebrew) is not the most common title in Mark, its use in 1:1 seems to indicate that it is the fundamental way in which Mark presents Jesus, employed as it is by Peter in his pivotal confession in 8:29. In three places, Jesus uses it, albeit somewhat obliquely, to refer to himself. In 9:41 he refers to the disciples as those who "belong to Christ." In 12:35 he poses the question whether the Christ is merely the "son" of David. In 13:21 he warns the disciples not to be deceived if people tell them that the Christ has come. The final two occurrences of the title are used by others at his trial and crucifixion. In 14:61 the high priest asks Jesus if he is "the Christ, the Son of the Blessed," and Jesus responds that he is (14:62). In 15:32 the chief priests and scribes mock Jesus by challenging "the Christ, the King of Israel" to come down from the cross so that they might believe.

This final instance equates "Christ" and "King of Israel." Although in the Old Testament priests (e.g., Ex. 28:41) and prophets (e.g., 1 Kings 19:16) were anointed, the term *messiah* in the world of first-century Judaism primarily referred to kings, who were also anointed (e.g., 1 Sam. 15:1).[3] The expectation of a messiah par excellence (see 1 Sam. 2:35) was primarily an expectation of an anointed king who would crush God's enemies and rule the nations (Ps. 2:2). In the first century,

---

2   Some express considerable doubt concerning whether "Son of God" in 1:1 is original since it is missing in some very significant early manuscripts. For the sake of this work, I cautiously assume the phrase's inclusion. For a succinct argument for its originality, see Robert A. Guelich, *Mark 1–8:26*, WBC (Dallas: Word, 1989), 6.

3   M. Eugene Boring, *Mark: A Commentary*, NTL (Louisville: Westminster John Knox, 2006), 249.

messiah language, though diverse,[4] does speak to a specific problem: "determining who is and who should be in charge."[5] Although the term is uniquely Jewish and Christian, "Persians, Greeks, Romans, and others had their own ways of talking"[6] about unique leaders who would come and "inaugurate a new and better order."[7]

However, in presenting the Christ as dying on the cross, Mark narrates something unheard of: a messiah or Christ who *suffers*. This did not cohere with the anticipation of the triumphant, all-conquering king inside or outside of Judaism. Peter's rebuke of Jesus reflects the incongruity of a suffering messiah (Mark 8:31–32). As Paul puts it, the notion of a crucified Christ was "a stumbling block to Jews and folly to Gentiles" (1 Cor. 1:23). Paul's gospel, which centered on "Jesus Christ and him crucified" (1 Cor. 2:2), thus finds its origins in the life and teaching of Jesus himself.

Jesus's identity as Christ is, however, one aspect where we see a difference between Paul and Mark. In Mark's Gospel, Jesus is reluctant to take this identity upon himself, whereas in Paul's letters it is by far the most common way for him to refer to Jesus. We will see that twice Jesus interprets the title "Christ" by using "Son of Man" (Mark 8:29–31; 14:61–62), his preferred title. Son of Man (as we will see below) was not a title to which first-century people attached considerable expectation. By employing it, therefore, Jesus could more easily speak of himself without the misunderstanding and fervor that "Christ" might have generated.

This underlines Mark's historical agenda and reminds us that he is not merely writing theology. In writing of Jesus before the cross and

4   As Joshua W. Jipp, *The Messianic Theology of the New Testament* (Grand Rapids, MI: Eerdmans, 2020), 75, puts it, "There is no single meaning to *messiah* or messiah language."

5   Matthew V. Novenson, *The Grammar of Messianism: An Ancient Jewish Political Idiom and Its Users* (Oxford: Oxford University Press, 2017), 272.

6   Novenson, *Grammar*, 272.

7   Christian Habicht, "Messianic Elements in the Pre-Christian Greco Roman World," in *Toward the Millennium: Messianic Expectations from the Bible to Waco*, ed. Peter Shäfer and Mark R. Cohen, Studies in the History of Religions 77 (Leiden: Brill, 1988), 47 (cited in Novenson, *Grammar*, 272).

resurrection, Mark shows that Jesus wanted to downplay unhelpful expectations and stress his impending suffering and death, thus favoring Son of Man language. Paul, writing from the perspective of the resurrection, appropriately refers to Jesus as Christ—a title that speaks more universally to Jesus's exalted status. Nevertheless, Paul's language of "Christ and him crucified" underscores the point that this is not the Christ of popular expectation.

Son of God

Many argue that "Son of God" is the key title in Mark's Gospel.[8] God himself identifies Jesus as his Son at his baptism (1:11) and transfiguration (9:7), and demons (who are presumed to have supernatural knowledge)[9] twice address him as such (3:11; 5:7). Furthermore, the placement of this title at the beginning (1:1, 11), middle (9:7), and end (15:39) of the Gospel points to its significance for Mark.[10]

The two affirmations from God that Jesus is his Son evoke Psalm 2:7 ("You are my Son; today I have begotten you"), which, in turn, is a meditation on God's promise to David in 2 Samuel 7:14. As with "Christ," it seems that "Son of God" is primarily an expression of Jesus's kingship. Thus, "Mark's use of Messiah and 'Son of God' finds unity in the notion of God's appointed eschatological ruler."[11]

However, "Christ" and "Son of God," while both evoking the notion of kingship, do subtly differ from one another. If *Christ* was a particularly Jewish term, *Son of God* was one used by both Jews and Gentiles.[12] In the Old Testament the term *son* "not only had its usual biological meaning, but often designated the category to which someone or something belonged."[13] So in the Old Testament "son of God" could be used "for a being who belongs to the heavenly world"—that

---

8 See Adam Winn, *Reading Mark's Christology Under Caesar: Jesus the Messiah and Roman Imperial Ideology* (Downers Grove, IL: IVP Academic, 2018), 53.

9 Winn, *Reading Mark's Christology*, 53.

10 Winn, *Reading Mark's Christology*, 53.

11 Winn, *Reading Mark's Christology*, 53.

12 Boring, *Mark*, 250.

13 Boring, *Mark*, 250.

is, an angel (e.g., Job 1:6). It could be used of Israel (e.g., Ex. 4:22) and of kings (e.g., Ps. 2:7), the nation or person that particularly belonged to God. In the New Testament, it is used of Christians (e.g., Matt. 5:9; Rom. 8:14). In Jewish contexts, a human being could be designated "son of God" in an unremarkable way—meaning they belonged to God. However, in Gentile thought, the term had a more supernatural flavor, in that kings and rulers were understood to be sons of the gods in a more particular sense. This gives irony to the centurion's confession of Jesus as Son of God (Mark 15:39), a "title that a Roman soldier would normally attribute to the Roman emperor."[14]

"Son of God" as a title, then, can point to Jesus's divine identity, but it raises the question, what type of divine identity? Roman emperors were *made* (i.e., declared to be) gods by the people following their achievements. As such, they were not regarded as gods in the same way that, say, Jupiter was. They were not understood as gods by nature or as preexistent gods. What *kind* of deity, if any, does Jesus possess by virtue of being the Son of God? Some commentators suggest that Jesus *became* Son of God at his baptism—that is, he was *adopted* as Son of God in a manner *somewhat* analogous to a Roman emperor. They point to similar language in Romans 1:4 where it has been argued that Paul is teaching that Jesus *became* Son of God following his resurrection. However, this is a misreading of Paul since in the previous verse Paul has already identified Jesus as God's Son at his birth (Rom. 1:3).[15]

Indicators in Mark's Gospel show that, like Paul, Mark has a *stronger* view of Jesus's deity and considers him to be the *preexistent* Son of God.[16] Prior to the declaration of his sonship at his baptism, Jesus does not perform any miracles or do anything that would *merit* his adoption as Son. That is, the declaration of his sonship at the beginning of the narrative suggests that Jesus is *recognized* rather than *made* Son of God.

14 Michael F. Bird, *Jesus is the Christ: The Messianic Testimony of the Gospels* (Downers Grove, IL: IVP Academic, 2012), 52.

15 On this, see Peter Orr, *Exalted Above the Heavens: The Risen and Ascended Christ*, NSBT (Downers Grove, IL: IVP Academic, 2018), 31–35.

16 Michael F. Bird, *Jesus the Eternal Son: Answering Adoptionist Christology* (Grand Rapids, MI: Eerdmans, 2017), 82.

Furthermore, the fact that Jesus is recognized as Son of God by God himself and other supernatural beings (Mark 3:11) suggests that he is not merely a "temporary" (i.e., recent) "visitor to the heavenly council, like the prophets, but rather a *permanent* member."[17]

The high priest seems to understand this strong claim to deity inherent in the title "Son of God" when he asks Jesus if he is the "Son of the Blessed [i.e., of God]" in 14:61 (we will return to this complex interaction below). Jesus's affirmation that he is the Son of the Blessed is met with the charge of blasphemy. Jesus claims that he is "the Son of God on a level with God and with divine authority."[18]

The term *Son of God* for Mark, in addition to pointing to Jesus's royal identity (overlapping as it does with *Christ*), is a strong indicator of his deity.

Son of Man

Between Peter's confession that Jesus is the Christ (8:29) and his rebuke of Jesus for suggesting that he should die (8:32), Jesus does two things. He commands the disciples to be silent, and he teaches them that the Son of Man would suffer and die (8:30–31). This subtle change in title ("Christ" in 8:29 to "Son of Man" in 8:31) suggests that the titles are not hermetically sealed from one another. Although Jesus speaks of his suffering in terms of the Son of Man, he does so in response to Peter's confession of the Christ.

This is a title, like Christ, that is uniquely Jewish and Christian. It follows the sense of "son of God" in belonging to a category—that is, a son of man is a human being, someone who belongs to the category of "man."[19] This prosaic usage is seen in places such as Numbers 23:19; Psalm 8:4; and Ezekiel 2:1. However, the term seems to have a more specific reference in Daniel 7 where a "son of man" is presented before

---

17 Simon Gathercole, *The Preexistent Son: Recovering the Christologies of Matthew, Mark, and Luke* (Grand Rapids, MI: Eerdmans, 2006), 206 (emphasis in original).

18 David E. Garland, *A Theology of Mark's Gospel: Good News about Jesus the Messiah, the Son of God*, Biblical Theology of the New Testament (Grand Rapids, MI: Zondervan Academic, 2015), 241.

19 Boring, *Mark*, 251.

God ("the Ancient of Days") and given "dominion and glory and a kingdom, that all peoples, nations, and languages should serve him" (Dan. 7:13–14).

Although Son of Man is clearly a biblical image and even though Daniel views the figure as an eschatological agent to come, there was not a widespread expectation of a coming Son of Man figure in Second Temple Judaism. As I argued above, Jesus may have deliberately chosen the term to refer to himself because it would not have created the same expectations as "Son of God" or "Christ." Reading across Mark's Gospel, we see that Jesus uses the title in three particular contexts: referring to his return (8:38; 13:26; 14:62); to his authority (2:10, 28); and to his suffering, death, and resurrection (8:31; 9:9, 12, 31; 10:33–34; 10:45; 14:21, 41).[20]

Perhaps the most significant use of this title is found in his trial when the high priest asks Jesus if he is "the Christ, the Son of the Blessed" (14:61). Jesus affirms that he is but then says that they "will see the *Son of Man* seated at the right hand of Power, and coming with the clouds of heaven" (14:62). In his answer, Jesus combines the language of Daniel 7:13 ("with the clouds of heaven there came one like a son of man") and Psalm 110:1 ("sit at my right hand") to point to his role as a heavenly judge who will share the very throne of God. He will exercise "divine power" since he shares "equality with God."[21] The one who is on trial will one day judge the world as the divine Son of Man.

Jesus's identity as Son of Man sharpens some of the seeming tensions we have already seen in Mark's presentation of Jesus. He is a real human being *and* one who shares equality with God: man and God. He is one who will possess glory and honor but also one who will suffer and die as a ransom for many. The term also neatly reflects the hiddenness-revelation motif in the Gospel (that I will examine in chapter 2). It conceals Jesus's identity in the sense that it does not create the same sense of expectation that "Christ" or "Son of God" would. However,

---

20 Boring, *Mark*, 251.
21 Garland, *A Theology of Mark's Gospel*, 240.

the term reveals as well as conceals. For those who have "ears to hear" (4:9), the term speaks of Jesus's authority and glory.

Lord

The title "lord" (*kyrios*) can refer to a master or be used as a polite address akin to the English "sir." However, in the Bible it carries particular importance since the Septuagint uses *kyrios* to render the Hebrew divine name "Yahweh" (often "LORD" in English translations of the Old Testament).

On several occasions, Jesus is addressed as "Lord" when it seems to be used simply as a term of polite address (e.g., 7:28; cf. 11:3). Of more interest is where the term seems to refer both to God and Jesus. In 1:3 Mark quotes Isaiah 40:3, which calls for people to prepare for the "Lord"—that is, God in the original context (Isa. 40:3: "prepare the way of the LORD; make straight in the desert a highway for our God"). To apply this text to Jesus implies that, at least on some level, God and Jesus can be identified.

Jesus describes himself, the Son of Man, as "lord even of the Sabbath" in Mark 2:28. This is not a formal title used in the Old Testament, but Exodus 20:11 declares that "the LORD blessed the Sabbath day and made it holy." Again, this suggests that Jesus's description of himself in Mark 2:28 is an implicit claim to deity. When Jesus dramatically heals the demon-possessed man whom "no one could bind" (Mark 5:3), Jesus tells him, "Go home to your friends and tell them how much the Lord has done for you" (5:19). The man goes on his way, and Mark says he "began to proclaim in the Decapolis how much *Jesus* had done for him" (5:20). In 12:36–37 Jesus corrects the scribes' view that the Christ is a mere descendent of David. He points out that in Psalm 110:1, David "in the Holy Spirit" calls him "Lord." Furthermore, God invites him to share his heavenly throne with the words "sit at my right hand" (12:36). The Christ, then, is David's Lord and shares the heavenly throne of God. In the Old Testament and in Jewish Second Temple literature, only God sits on the throne in heaven. Human agents may rule on behalf of God *on earth,* but they never share God's throne in heaven. By applying this psalm to himself, Jesus is making the exalted claim that, in Richard Bauckham's language, he is included in the "unique divine identity."[22]

Although not as frequent as some of the other titles, "Lord," then, is a Christologically significant title. It is also a central title for Paul, especially in his formulation that "Jesus is Lord" (Rom. 10:9; 1 Cor. 12:3; Phil. 2:11). For Paul, as for Mark, the attribution of the title "Lord" to Jesus points to his divine identity (cf. Rom. 10:12; 1 Cor 8:6).[23]

Teacher

By far the most common title for Jesus in Mark's Gospel is "Teacher," which occurs on the lips of the disciples (4:38; 9:38; 10:35; 13:1), of those in the crowd who interact with Jesus (5:35; 9:17; 10:17; 10:20), and of the Jewish leaders (12:14, 19, 32). Jesus refers to himself as "Teacher" in 14:14. The related Greek terms *rabbi* (9:5; 11:21; 14:45) and *rabbouni* (10:51)—both rendered in the ESV as "Rabbi"—are also used. The verb "to teach" (*didaskō*) is used seventeen times in Mark, with all but two instances referring to Jesus's activity (1:21, 22; 2:13; 4:1, 2; 6:2, 6, 34; 8:31; 9:31; 10:1; 11:17; 12:14, 35; 14:49). The noun "teaching" (*didachē*) is used five times (1:22, 27; 4:2; 11:18; 12:38) to describe the activity of Jesus.

Unlike Matthew, Mark does not give us sustained blocks of Jesus's teaching. Rather, Jesus's periodic teaching in Mark seems to function to highlight his authority. In 1:21–28, we encounter Jesus teaching in a synagogue where the people are astonished since "he taught them as one who had authority, and not as the scribes" (1:22). While in the synagogue, he drives out a demon by speaking, and again the people respond with astonishment ("What is this?") as they recognize a "new teaching with authority" (1:27). Jesus's identity as teacher is not simply an educational or instructional role but a function of his authority as one sent by God. In fact, the authority of Jesus's words points to his

---

22 See Richard Bauckham, "Is 'High Human Christology' Sufficient? A Critical Response to J. R. Daniel Kirk's *A Man Attested by God*," *BBR* 27, no. 4 (2017): 508–9.

23 See Gordon Fee, *Pauline Christology: An Exegetical-Theological Study* (Peabody, MA: Hendrickson, 2007), 558–85.

divine authority since although heaven and earth will pass way, his words "will not pass away" (13:31).[24]

Scholars commonly observe that not much of Jesus's teaching features in the letters of Paul. However, there are significant parallels between Jesus's teaching in Mark and some major issues in Paul's letters, namely, divorce (Mark 10:2–9; 1 Cor. 7:10–11), honoring the emperor (Mark 12:13–17; Rom. 13:1–8), and the great command to love (Mark 12:30–31; 1 Cor. 13:13; Rom. 13:8–9).[25]

Other Titles

Other titles used of Jesus include "prophet," used by Jesus of himself (Mark 6:4) and by the people trying to understand him (6:15; cf. 8:28); "shepherd," which appears in the Zechariah 13:7 quotation that Jesus applied to himself in Mark 14:27 (cf. 6:34); "holy one of God," spoken by the demons (1:24); and "bridegroom," an Old Testament image expressing God's relationship to Israel that Jesus applied to himself (2:19–20).

The significant title "King of the Jews" is used five times in the context of his crucifixion (15:2, 9, 12, 18, 26), and the related "King of Israel" (in parallel with "Christ") is used by the chief priests and scribes when Jesus hangs on the cross (15:32). Bartimaeus, a blind beggar, calls Jesus "Son of David" as he cries out for mercy (10:47, 48), and Jesus uses the same expression to correct a misunderstanding—that the Christ was merely an earthly descendent of David (12:35). In contrast, as we have seen, he reminds the temple audience that David calls the Christ "my Lord" (12:36, citing Ps. 110:1). His throne is not merely the one in Jerusalem but at God's right hand.[26]

Mark's narrative gives shape to how we are to understand Jesus even as it expresses some of the *apparent* contradictions in Mark's

---

24 Bird, *Jesus the Eternal Son*, 99.

25 Margaret Mitchell, "Mark, the Long-Form Pauline εὐαγγέλιον," in *Modern and Ancient Literary Criticism of the Gospels: Continuing the Debate on Gospel Genre(s)*, ed. R. M. Calhoun, D. P. Moessner, and T. Nicklas, WUNT 451 (Tübingen: Mohr Siebeck, 2020), 216.

26 So Joel Marcus, *The Way of the Lord: Christological Exegesis of the Old Testament in the Gospel of Mark* (Louisville: Westminster John Knox, 1992), 151.

Christology—that is, portraying him as both "the powerful, truly divine Son of God" and as "truly human, fully identified with human weakness and victimization."[27] The different titles used of Jesus are not actually contradictory but bring out the different aspects of his singular identity.[28] The three dominant themes that emerge are authority, glory, and suffering. These are held together especially in the title that Jesus most frequently uses of himself, "Son of Man."

I have noted that 14:61–62 contains three titles: Christ, Son of [God], and Son of Man. As Michael Bird strikingly puts it, these verses act as something of a "christological blender, with the major titles driven together and defined by each other."[29] The terms are not collapsed into one another but are "pressed into the definition created by Mark's overarching narrative of the Messiah commissioned to enact God's reign and to die a martyr's death on the cross."[30] Even more than that, this human agent of God is also the one who shares his throne as "Lord" and "Son." The titles of Jesus do more than point to his divine identity, but they certainly do not do less—something that is underlined when we consider his miracles.

Jesus's Miracles and His Divine Identity

By providing a narrative of Jesus's life, Mark can *show* what Paul can only *state*. This is particularly relevant when we consider Jesus's divine identity. While Paul affirms or assumes the deity of Christ in his letters (e.g., Rom. 9:5; Phil. 2:5–11; 1 Cor. 8:6),[31] Mark can portray Jesus doing what only God can do. Perhaps most obvious is his healing of the paralytic in Mark 2:1–12. Before healing this man, who had been lowered on a mat before him, Jesus tells him that his sins are forgiven (2:5). The onlooking scribes question Jesus's words, asking, "Who can forgive sins but God alone?" (2:7). Knowing their thoughts, Jesus

---

27 Boring, *Mark*, 258.

28 Winn, *Reading Mark's Christology*, 60.

29 Bird, *Jesus is the Christ*, 51.

30 Bird, *Jesus is the Christ*, 51.

31 On this see Chris Tilling, *Paul's Divine Christology*, WUNT 2.323 (Tübingen: Mohr Siebeck, 2012).

proceeds to heal the paralytic, thus demonstrating that "the Son of Man has authority on earth to forgive sins" (2:10).

This miracle pulls us into the debate concerning Jesus's deity. There is no *explicit* statement of Jesus's deity in Mark like we have in John 1:1 ("the Word was God"). However, we do have accounts in Mark where Jesus does what only God can do, such as forgive sins, calm a storm (4:35–41), and provide food for thousands of people (6:30–44; 8:1–10). Debate centers on whether Jesus does these miracles because he *is* God, or because he has received power and authority *from* God. If we return to the healing of the paralytic, Jesus does not say that the healing demonstrates his deity but that, as the Son of Man, he has authority on earth to forgive sins.

J. Daniel Kirk presents a strong argument for the view that Mark presents Jesus exclusively as a human being (albeit an "idealized" one). For Kirk, "Mark draws us to recognize in the character of Jesus a specially designated human person embodying the divine prerogatives rather than a human embodiment of Israel's God."[32] Or more sharply, "authority to act for God, even in the divine prerogative of establishing forgiveness of sins, does not indicate ontological divinity or preexistence."[33]

Kirk's volume is certainly correct in what it affirms: the Jesus of Mark's Gospel *is* presented as an idealized human being, the human being par excellence. However, is Kirk correct in what he denies? Is it true that Mark does not view Jesus as divine?

To answer this question, I will examine three of the more spectacular nature miracles in Mark's Gospel and consider whether Mark presents Jesus as actually sharing the characteristics of God and whether people relate to him as God.[34] I will return to the healing of the paralytic at the end.

---

32   J. R. Daniel Kirk, *A Man Attested by God: The Human Jesus of the Synoptic Gospels* (Grand Rapids, MI: Eerdmans, 2016), 263.

33   Kirk, *A Man Attested by God*, 279.

34   These two aspects are modified from Beniamin Pascut, *Redescribing Jesus's Divinity through A Social Science Theory*, WUNT 2.438 (Tübingen: Mohr Siebeck, 2017).

Jesus Calms a Storm (4:35–41)

The greatness of the miracle is clear—Jesus calms a great windstorm with just his words (4:37–39). His control over the sea, as has often been noted, matches the control that Yahweh demonstrates in the exodus. However, debate centers on whether Jesus is acting *as* God or as one who has received power and authority *from* God.

First, consider what Jesus does. It seems irrefutable that Jesus is acting *as* God, doing what no other human figure in history has done. He does not simply pray to God; he acts as God. He rebukes the wind and the sea just as God was said to do at the exodus. Psalm 106:9 (Ps. 105:9 LXX) celebrates how God "rebuked [*epetimēsen*] the Red Sea, and it became dry." In Mark 4:39, Jesus "rebuked [*epetimēsen*] the wind" and spoke to the sea before it became calm. The disciples respond in amazement, asking, "Who then is this, that even the wind and the sea obey him?" (4:41). Psalm 107 declares that God "made the storm be still, and the waves of the sea were hushed" (Ps. 107:29). As Richard Hays puts it, "For any reader versed in Israel's Scripture, there can be only one possible answer: it is the Lord God of Israel who has the power to command wind and sea and to subdue the chaotic forces of nature."[35]

Nevertheless, Kirk points to Psalm 89. The Lord celebrates the ideal son of David—the one whom he has anointed and strengthened (Ps. 89:20–21), the one whom God will make "the firstborn, the highest of the kings of the earth" (Ps. 89:27). Furthermore, because of their unique relationship, God also promises this Davidic king that he "will set his hand on the sea and his right hand on the rivers" (Ps. 89:25). Controlling the chaos of the sea, Kirk argues, is certainly "divine power, but Psalm 89 shows that even in this particular, God is capable of extending this power such that it is embodied in a human agent."[36] Similarly, in Exodus 14:16 the Lord tells Moses to "stretch out your hand over the sea and divide it" (cf. Ex. 14:26). Jesus, it seems, is acting in a way that is consistent with the Old Testament understanding of the unique

---

35 Richard B. Hays, *Reading Backwards: Figural Christology and the Fourfold Gospel Witness* (Waco, TX; Baylor University Press, 2014), 22 (cited in Kirk, *A Man Attested by God*, 441).

36 Kirk, *A Man Attested by God*, 441.

leader of his people—he is given control over the wind and the waves *by God* not because he is God himself.

Is Jesus doing anything more than Moses did in Exodus 14:16 or that God promised his eschatological king would do in Psalm 89:25? To answer this, we need to consider how Jesus expects his disciples to respond to him.

In favor of Jesus acting as God's *representative*, it is argued that his rebuke of the disciples in Mark 4:40 is for their lack of faith. And faith, Jesus will later teach, is directed toward *God* (11:22). The implication being that if the disciples had trusted *God,* they too would have been able to calm the storm.[37]

However, faith in Mark is also directed toward *Christ*. In 2:5 Jesus responds to the faith of the friends of the paralytic—a faith that is clearly directed to him and his power to heal their friend.[38] In 5:34 the woman who has just been healed by Jesus from her continual discharge of blood is commended by Jesus for her faith, which had been directed toward him: "Your faith has made you well." We see the same in the encounter with the blind man who called out, "Son of David, have mercy on me!" (10:48). Jesus tells him, "Your faith has made you well" (10:52). Once again, faith is directed toward Jesus. In 5:36 Jesus tells the synagogue ruler with the dying daughter not to fear but to believe—presumably in Jesus. In 6:6 Jesus is amazed by the faithlessness of his fellow townspeople—a lack of faith arising from their failure to understand who Jesus is. The father of a demon-possessed boy asks Jesus to help him "if [he] can do anything" (9:22). Jesus gently rebukes him: "All things are possible for one who believes." Again, the object of faith is Jesus himself. The man responds by asking Jesus to help him believe (9:24)—something only God can do. In 9:42 he issues a severe warning to anyone who "causes one of these little ones who believe *in me* to sin."

---

37 Joanna Dewey, "The Markan Jesus, Jesus's Actions, And the Kingdom of God," in *Let the Reader Understand: Essays in Honor of Elizabeth Struthers Malbon*, ed. Edwin K. Broadhead, LNTS 583 (London: T&T Clark, 2018), 73.

38 Eckhard J. Schnabel, *Mark: An Introduction and Commentary*, TNTC (Downers Grove, IL: IVP Academic, 2017), 115.

Certainly, Jesus teaches the appropriateness of faith in God in 11:22, which he expands in 11:23–25 in terms of *prayer*; however, the more frequent object of faith in Mark's Gospel is Jesus himself. Of course, Jesus directs people to a right understanding of, trust in, and worship of God (7:7). It is, however, inaccurate to say that Jesus "insistently proclaims not himself but God."[39] Again, it might be true that faith is directed toward Jesus as God's representative, but Mark claims so much more. He is narrating what Jesus implies in John 14:1—if you believe in Jesus, you believe in God.

What Jesus does (calms the storm) and how he expects his disciples to react (have faith in him), declare his divine nature. He is the fulfill-ment of Israel's eschatological hope (Ps. 89:25) but also the one whom people relate to as they relate to God. In fact, Psalm 89 confesses of God himself, "You rule the raging of the sea; when its waves rise, you still them" (Ps 89:9). As we will see in the next two miracles, in Jesus's actions there is a fusing of identity between the eschatological agent and God himself.

Jesus Feeds the Five Thousand (6:30–44)

In perhaps one of the most famous miracles in Mark's Gospel, Jesus provides food for a crowd of five thousand men together with women and children. The crowd has tracked down Jesus and his disciples. He spends the rest of the day teaching them because, Mark tells us, "he had compassion on them, because they were like sheep without a shepherd" (6:34). At the end of the day, his disciples suggest that the people need to be sent away to the surrounding villages to buy something to eat (6:36). Jesus responds by telling the disciples to give the crowd something to eat. This is impossible, so they reply, "Shall we go and buy two hundred denarii worth of bread and give it to them to eat?" (6:37). When Jesus learns that they have five loaves and two fish, he has the crowd sit in groups (6:38–40). Then, taking these loaves and fish, "he looked up to

---

39 Elizabeth S. Malbon, *Mark's Jesus: Characterization as Narrative Christology* (Waco, TX: Baylor University Press, 2009), 216.

heaven and said a blessing and broke the loaves and gave them to the disciples to set before the people. And he divided the two fish among them all" (6:41). Mark tells us that everyone ate and was satisfied and that twelve basketfuls of bread and fish were left over (6:42–43).

The description of the crowd as being "like sheep without a shepherd" (6:34) may be, as is often argued, an allusion to Numbers 27 where Moses, in the face of his own death, prays to the Lord to appoint "a man over the congregation" who will lead the people so that "the congregation of the LORD may not be as sheep that have no shepherd" (Num. 27:16–17). The Lord answers the prayer by telling Moses to take "Joshua the son of Nun, a man in whom is the Spirit, and lay your hand on him" (Num. 27:18).

For Kirk, this passage depicts Jesus as a "royal Moses figure."[40] Like Moses, he is the one who "shepherds shepherdless Israel in the wilderness by teaching the people (v. 34) and ultimately by feeding the people by the hands of his disciples and the miraculous provision of bread (vv. 39–44)."[41] The connection to David may not be as close to the surface, but the promise of "superabundant provision of food with the restoration of David's line" in Amos 9:11–15 points in that direction.[42] What Jesus does, he does as a human being. This is underlined by the fact that the disciples share in the miracle too by distributing the bread and the fish (as they do with the bread in the parallel miracle in 8:1–9). Jesus "does not reserve this miracle for himself as one indicating his unique divine authority or ontology, but instead extends the authority to his disciples as those capable of doing the same."[43]

Kirk concludes,

> Mark is not here introducing a new, divine Christology such that Jesus is playing the role of divine shepherd as such (e.g., Ps. 23; Ezek. 34:11–16) but is instead building on the high human Christol-

---

40 Kirk, *A Man Attested by God*, 452.
41 Kirk, *A Man Attested by God*, 452.
42 Kirk, *A Man Attested by God*, 452.
43 Kirk, *A Man Attested by God*, 454.

ogy where the faithful human king represents the divine shepherd through his tending of the flock (e.g., Ezek. 34:23–24).[44]

Perhaps most strikingly is the parallel with Elisha in 2 Kings 4:42–44 where Elisha provided bread for a hundred men so that there were leftovers.[45]

However, is Mark presenting Jesus as *more* than the fulfillment of these eschatological expectations? Adela Yarbro Collins notes several ways in which Jesus's actions amplify what Elisha does. First, the magnitude of the miracle is greater. Elisha takes twenty loaves to feed one hundred people, while Jesus takes five loaves and two fish to feed five thousand people. Second, as Collins puts it, "God plays a more direct role in the Elisha story."[46] He sends Elisha, and as he performs the miracle, Elisha instructs his servant, "For thus says the LORD" (2 Kings 4:43). The narrator concludes that the miracle was done "according to the word of the LORD" (4:44). In Jesus's case, although we do read of him looking to heaven and saying a blessing, "there is little indication that the miracle is God's rather than Jesus's."[47]

It is right to see Jesus fulfilling the Old Testament expectations of Moses/Joshua (Num. 27:17), David (Ezek. 34:1–31), and Elisha (2 Kings 4:23–24).[48] But even in the Old Testament, the expectation is that God himself will shepherd his people. We saw earlier that the citation of Isaiah 40:3 in Mark 1:2–3 orients us to the expectation that the coming one will be God himself. A few verses later, Isaiah promises that the Lord God will come "with might" (Isa. 40:10) and that he will "tend his flock like a shepherd" (40:11). The expectation of a coming human shepherd is combined with the expectation of God himself coming. We see a similar dynamic in Ezekiel 34:8–18 where the Lord himself

---

44 Kirk, *A Man Attested by God*, 453.
45 For a discussion of the parallels, see Adela Yarbro Collins, *Mark: A Commentary on the Gospel of Mark*, Hermeneia (Minneapolis: Fortress, 2007), 320.
46 Collins, *Mark*, 320.
47 Collins, *Mark*, 320.
48 See James R. Edwards, *The Gospel according to Mark*, PNTC (Grand Rapids, MI: Eerdmans, 2002), 195.

promises that he will come and shepherd his people: "I myself will be the shepherd of my sheep" (Ezek. 34:15). However, he will also "set up over them one shepherd, my servant David, and he shall feed them: he shall feed them and be their shepherd" (Ezek. 34:23). The Old Testament anticipates that both the Lord and the eschatological David will shepherd the people. Certainly, the characteristic of having compassion on his people is one that God himself displays throughout the Old Testament.[49]

When we combine the greatness of the miracle, the Old Testament expectation of the Lord himself coming as shepherd, and the indication in Mark 1:2 that Jesus himself fulfills the expectation of this divine coming, it seems that there "is little question that for Mark, in some mysterious way the great shepherd Yahweh is himself present in Jesus."[50]

Jesus Walks on Water (6:45–52)

Jesus walks across the sea of Galilee to join the disciples in their boat as they row against a strong wind, making slow progress. When the disciples see Jesus, they cry out in terror, thinking he is a ghost (6:48–49). He reassures them and then enters the boat, and as he does so, the wind ceases (6:50–51). Mark adds a postscript to the effect that the disciples were "utterly astounded" because "they did not understand about the loaves, but their hearts were hardened" (6:51–52).

By walking on water, Jesus does what only God can do. Reflecting on the exodus, Isaiah describes the Lord as the one "who makes a way in the sea, a path in the mighty waters" (Isa. 43:16).[51] However, while the exodus involved Israel walking through the waters *on* dry land, Jesus is here walking *on* water.[52] Job describes *God* as the one who

---

49 Rikk E. Watts cites the following texts as examples: Ex. 33:19; Deut. 30:3; Isa. 14:1; 49:10, 13, 15; 54:8; 55:7; 60:10; Jer. 12:15; 30:18; 33:26; 42:12; Ezek. 39:25; Hos. 1:6–7; 2:23. See his "Mark," in *Commentary on the New Testament Use of the Old Testament*, ed. G. K. Beale and D. A. Carson (Grand Rapids, MI: Baker Academic, 2007), 161.

50 Watts, "Mark," 161.

51 Pointed out by Mark L. Strauss, *Mark*, ZECNT (Grand Rapids, MI: Zondervan Academic, 2014), 285.

52 Richard B. Hays, *Echoes of Scripture in the Gospels* (Waco, TX: Baylor University Press, 2016), 70.

alone "trampled the waves of the sea" (Job 9:8). Jesus's reassurance of the disciples in Mark 6:50 ("it is I") is the simple Greek phrase "I am" (*egō eimi*). No doubt this could be Jesus simply identifying himself, but in such a charged scene it may have more Christological significance, evoking God's own description of himself in Exodus 3:14, "I AM WHO I AM," which is alluded to elsewhere in the Old Testament (e.g., Deut. 32:39; Isa. 41:4; 51:12). Thus, "when Jesus speaks this same phrase, 'I am,' in his sea-crossing epiphany, it serves to underscore the claim of divine identity that is implicitly present in the story as a whole."[53]

There is also a detail in the text that seems superfluous. In 6:48 Mark tells us that Jesus "meant to pass by them." In Exodus 34:6 the Lord "passed before" Moses in the cloud as he revealed his character to him. In 1 Kings 19:11, as Elijah hides from Ahab and Jezebel in a cave, "the LORD passed by."[54] Perhaps the most intriguing possible allusion is Job's description of the Lord as the one who "passes by me," followed by a confession of his inability to understand God:

> Behold, he passes by me, and I see him not;
> he moves on, but I do not perceive him. (Job 9:11)

This inability to correctly perceive God parallels the disciples' inability to understand (Mark 6:52) and "accords deeply with Mark's emphasis on the elusiveness of the divine presence in Jesus."[55]

I could consider other miracles (e.g., raising Jairus's daughter from the dead in 5:41–42), but the ones we have looked at are sufficient to see that in addition to presenting Jesus as the fulfillment of Israel's eschatological and messianic hopes, Mark depicts him in some elusive way (to borrow Hays's language) as the Lord himself who has come to save his people.

We need to briefly return to Mark 2, for this is the passage that Kirk presses most strongly in suggesting that Mark does *not* present Jesus

---

53 Hays, *Echoes of Scripture in the Gospels*, 73.
54 See Collins, *Mark*, 334.
55 Hays, *Echoes of Scripture in the Gospels*, 72.

as divine. The scribes object that only God can forgive sins (2:7), and Jesus proves them wrong by healing the paralytic and demonstrating that he, the Son of Man, *also* has the authority to forgive sins. In other words, according to Kirk, Jesus corrects them not by asserting his deity but by showing that they have an overly narrow view of who can forgive.[56] However, the scribes are correct—this kind of forgiveness *is* the purview of God alone. Jesus is not doing what John the Baptist did—merely declaring that forgiveness is available (1:4).[57] Rather, he is sovereignly declaring this man's sins to be forgiven. That is, Jesus is not simply forgiving offenses committed against him personally. The scribes are correct: Jesus assumes the position of deity. Therefore, "once one grants that Jesus offers genuine forgiveness to the paralytic in the place of God (v. 10), then one must also conclude that there is an overlap in identity between Jesus and God."[58]

Conclusion

This chapter may feel like a ground clearing exercise. We have to deal with the person of Jesus in terms of his titles and the question of his deity. However, for two reasons this chapter has done more than just get this topic out of the way, so to speak. First, every other theme I consider in this book is connected to and ultimately derived from this fundamental theme of who Jesus is. We would not be interested in what Mark says about the death of Jesus if we are not first convinced of the identity of Jesus.

Second, Jesus's person is central to Mark not simply because he is the main character but because of the way that Mark frames his work—the gospel of Jesus Christ, the Son of God. In framing his work as articulating the *beginning* of the gospel, he then immediately qualifies the gospel as being about Jesus Christ. The only other time the word

---

56 Kirk, *A Man Attested*, 278–79. Kirk writes, "In this first story about Jesus's authority Mark does not mean to tell us that Jesus is, in fact, divine in some proto-Chalcedonian sense" (278).

57 A point made by Kirk, *A Man Attested*, 274–75.

58 Pascut, *Redescribing Jesus's Divinity*, 191.

"gospel" is clarified with a genitive phrase (as here) is in 1:14 when Mark tells us that Jesus went into the region of Galilee, proclaiming "the gospel of God." There is a parallel with the beginning of Romans. Paul describes himself as set apart for the "gospel of God" (Rom. 1:1), which is "concerning his Son" (1:3). Paul is an apostle of God's gospel that concerns his Son. Mark writes the beginning of the gospel of God concerning Jesus Christ, the Son of God. Mark and Paul not only share an understanding of how the gospel relates to both God and Jesus but also an understanding of Jesus's divine identity. Mark's conception of "Jesus' pre-existence as a *divine son*"[59] who comes into the world matches Paul's conviction in Romans and elsewhere (cf. Rom. 8:3; 10:6; Gal. 4:4; Phil. 2:6–8 etc.).[60]

However, in sharing these convictions about Jesus's identity, Mark is not simply replicating what Paul says in his letters. We have seen that Mark reflects the historical situation of Jesus's ministry and his preference for "Son of Man" to refer to himself (as opposed to Paul's more frequent use of "Christ"). This is a term that, I have argued, conceals as well as reveals. As we consider the topic of revelation in the next chapter, we see that this perfectly suits Jesus's agenda. He hides his identity from those on the *outside* and reveals it to those on the *inside*.

Mark's narrative portrays the identity of Jesus through Jesus's own words and actions. Yet, as we continue, we will see that the identity of Jesus is not only communicated through his words and actions but also through the words and actions of other people in response to Jesus.[61] This first chapter has only introduced the identity of Jesus. Each subsequent chapter, even as it touches on its own theme, will help us build a fuller picture of Mark's portrayal of Jesus.

---

59 Bird, *Jesus the Eternal Son*, 78.

60 See Gathercole, *Preexistent Son*, 23–45.

61 In *Mark's Jesus*, Malbon analyzes Mark's Christology through the following headings: "What Jesus Does," "What Others Say," "What Jesus Says in Response," "What Jesus Says Instead," and "What Others Do." Although I have not formally adopted this schema, I have tried to bear these different relationships in mind.

2

Revelation

Written, Proclaimed, Received

IN WRITING A BOOK THAT NARRATES the "beginning of the gospel," Mark frames his work in terms of *revelation*. The gospel is a *message* to be proclaimed. Following his baptism and temptation, the first thing that Jesus does is proclaim the gospel of God (Mark 1:14). Jesus has come as an agent of revelation—announcing God's message for the world and calling for repentance and belief in this message (1:15).

Mark weaves this theme of revelation throughout his Gospel; however, revelation is not a one-dimensional concept but is presented in a number of different modes across the book. Revelation in Mark is *written*, *proclaimed*, and *received*.

The second verse introduces the Scriptures, indicating that the revelation of the gospel (1:1) is grounded in the written Scriptures ("as it is written," 1:2). Throughout his book, Mark draws on the Old Testament to illuminate his picture of Jesus and his critique of Israel, particularly its leadership. Revelation in Mark's Gospel is *written*: the Old Testament is a source of revelation of the gospel of Jesus.

This first Scripture quotation is largely drawn from Isaiah 40:3 (see the discussion below). In addition to introducing the coming of the Lord, the text speaks of the messenger and his proclamation in the wilderness. Commentators often examine the theme of *silence* in Mark's

Gospel, noting Jesus's repeated commands not to speak about his miracles (e.g., Mark 1:44) or his identity (8:30). As a result, the theme of *proclamation* is frequently overlooked.[1] In the last chapter, we saw that the most common title applied to Jesus was "Teacher," and we will see that Jesus not only regularly teaches throughout the book but also expects his disciples to continue this activity. Revelation in Mark's Gospel is *proclaimed*: the gospel of Jesus is meant to be spoken and taught.

Another aspect of revelation is vital to Mark's presentation. In a key passage on the effect of the parables, Jesus speaks of those on the "outside" who "see but [do] not perceive" and "hear but [do] not understand" (4:12). Revelation is meant to be perceived and understood. This aspect of revelation relates to the heart. If people have hardened hearts, they have eyes but do not see and ears but do not hear (see 8:17–18). For revelation to be complete, eyes and ears must be opened and hearts softened. Accordingly, revelation in Mark's Gospel is not only grounded in Scripture (written) and proclaimed (spoken), it is also meant to be *received*.

As It Is Written

If I am correct to see the first verse in Mark to be the title of the work—*The Beginning of the Gospel about Jesus Christ, the Son of God*—then the work proper starts with a citation of Scripture:

As it is written in Isaiah the prophet,

"Behold, I send my messenger before your face,
who will prepare your way,
the voice of one crying in the wilderness:
'Prepare the way of the Lord,
make his paths straight.'" (1:2–3)

---

1   The connection between proclamation and discipleship was something I was first alerted to in Peter Ryan, "Promoting Proclamation: A Study of the Prominence, Content, and Rhetorical Impact of the Motif of Proclamation in the Gospel of Mark" (PhD thesis, Moore Theological College, 2021).

The first word of 1:2—*kathōs* in Greek, "as" in English—establishes a correspondence between the gospel (1:1) and Isaiah's words (1:2–3). Consider Mark 14:16 where we are told, "The disciples set out and went to the city and found it *just as* [*kathōs*] he had told them, and they prepared the Passover." What they found matched what Jesus had told them. There was a correspondence between Jesus's words and their experience. What is the nature of the correspondence between the gospel and what Isaiah wrote?

If the gospel in 1:1 is the proclaimed gospel of the apostles, particularly the apostle Paul, Mark is saying that this corresponds to the preaching that Isaiah predicted—preaching of a messenger before the coming of the Lord himself. John the Baptist (introduced in 1:4) is the messenger and Jesus is the Lord (i.e., Yahweh himself) promised in Isaiah 40:3.[2] In chapter 4 we will see that the context of Isaiah also establishes the framework of the salvation he brings (the Isaianic new exodus), but at this point it is enough to note that Mark flags at the outset the importance of the Old Testament for understanding the gospel about Jesus. In fact, Mark's narrative about Jesus is incomprehensible unless read against the Old Testament.

While in the past it was typical to downplay his use of Scripture, recent studies have highlighted Mark's sophisticated employment of the Old Testament. Mark, we will see, does more than *formally cite* Scripture (e.g., 1:2–3); he alludes to it throughout. Mark differs from the other Gospel writers in that rather than signposting his use of Scripture he is often "whispering to his readers" with his use of the Old Testament and inviting them to listen carefully.[3]

Mark, however, does occasionally point directly to the Scriptures to establish Jesus's identity (e.g., Ps. 110:1 in Mark 12:36), to explain the nature of his death (e.g., Zech. 13:7 in Mark 14:27), and to describe his

2   The precise syntactical relationship between 1:1 and 1:2 is complex. For a recent and comprehensive discussion of the issues, see Francesco Filannino, *The Theological Programme of Mark*, WUNT 2.551 (Tübingen: Mohr Siebeck, 2021), 13–66.

3   Richard B. Hays, *Echoes of Scripture in the Gospels* (Waco, TX: Baylor University Press, 2016), 15.

subsequent glory (Ps. 110:1 and Dan. 7:13 in Mark 14:62). Scripture citations are also used by Jesus to indict the Jewish leadership (e.g., 7:6–7; 11:17; 12:26).

Mark can also refer to Scripture in a summative, more wholistic way—that is, not to a particular Scripture but to the Scriptures as a whole. In 9:12, Jesus tells the disciples that it is "written of the Son of Man that he should suffer many things and be treated with contempt." In 14:21 Jesus states that "the Son of Man goes as it is written of him." In 14:49 Jesus knows his death will happen so that "the Scriptures [will] be fulfilled." As helpful as it is to consider possible Old Testament referents here (see the more detailed discussion in chapter 7), it is important not to obscure the point that Jesus is making—his death "is written in" and "fulfills" the Scriptures *as a whole*.

A subtle but nonetheless significant difference exists in how these two formula—"it is written" and "fulfillment" language—express the relationship between Jesus and the Scriptures. "Fulfillment" suggests that the event being narrated in some sense brings the antecedent Scripture to its completion. "It is written" essentially uses the Old Testament to *explain or prove the truthfulness* of an event. The Scriptures provide the background against which the event being narrated should be understood.[4] This second phrase in particular underlines the revelatory nature of Scripture. That is, to understand the death of the Son of Man, we have to understand what "is written" about his death. This is an invitation to a wholistic and broad consideration of the Scriptures—without ruling out particular Old Testament passages providing specific background.

I have already touched on Mark's use of Scripture in chapter 1, and I will return to it in the remaining chapters. At this stage, it is enough to notice the critical role that Scripture plays as a locus of revelation for Mark. It is impossible to understand Jesus without reading his life and death against the backdrop of the Old Testament.

---

4   To adapt the analysis of John's Gospel by Francis Maloney in "The Gospel of John as Scripture," *CBQ* 67 (2005): 454–68.

Proclamation and Silence

In 1901, the German biblical scholar William Wrede published *The Messianic Secret in the Gospels*, in which he considered Jesus's frequent commands to be silent in Mark's Gospel.[5] We see this occur twice in Mark 1. Jesus casts out many demons, and Mark tells us that he "would not permit the demons to speak, because they knew him" (1:34). Jesus then heals a man with a serious skin disease and "sternly charged him and sent him away at once" telling him to "say nothing to anyone" but only to make the offering that Moses commanded (1:43–44). Perhaps most strikingly, after Peter confesses that Jesus is the Christ, Jesus commands Peter and the other disciples "to tell no one about him" (8:29–30).

Wrede's explanation for this phenomenon is that Jesus did not understand himself to be the Messiah during his earthly ministry. The assertion that he was the Messiah was developed by the early church post-Easter. The notion of secrecy was then imposed on Mark's Gospel to explain this tension. Thus, if we ask, why did the early church think Jesus was the Messiah when he himself made no such claim? Mark, following early church tradition, explains this tension—contradiction even—by having Jesus silence people who recognized his messiahship.

Wrede's historical reconstruction has been thoroughly refuted, but his observation about Jesus frequently silencing demons and others continues to be discussed. Arguably this theme of *silence* has led commentators to overlook the importance of *proclamation* as a theme in Mark's Gospel.[6]

Following his baptism and temptation, Jesus proclaimed "the gospel of God" (1:14). In fact, Jesus defines his very mission in terms of preaching when he tells his disciples that he needs to keep moving to other towns, "that I may preach there also, for that is why I came out" (1:38). What does Jesus mean by "came out"? Does he refer to his leaving

---

5 William Wrede, *Das Messiasgeheimnis in den Evangelien: Zugleich ein Beitrag zum Verständnis des Markusevangeliums* (Göttingen: Vandenhoeck & Ruprecht, 1901). First published in English as *The Messianic Secret*, trans. James C. G. Grieg (Cambridge, UK: James Clarke, 1971).
6 This is the contention in Ryan, "Promoting Proclamation."

his current location of Capernaum (1:21) and traveling throughout all of Galilee (1:39)?[7] Or is it a reference to his mission from God—that he had been sent into the world to proclaim the gospel?[8] The immediate context does point to Jesus leaving Capernaum, but as R. T. France notes, the language of "coming" elsewhere in the Gospel (particularly 2:17 and 10:45) would lead "an instructed Christian reader" to understand the "coming" in 1:38 to convey "the concept of the 'coming into the world' of the pre-existent Son of God."[9] This is certainly how Luke understood the phrase: "I must preach the good news of the kingdom of God to the other towns as well; for I was sent for this purpose" (Luke 4:43). Jesus's entering the world as one sent by God is also a theme in John's Gospel and in Paul's letters (e.g., John 3:17; Gal. 4:4).

Jesus, then, understands proclaiming the gospel of the kingdom as essential to his mission. For all the commands to silence, Jesus has come to proclaim the gospel (Mark 1:14) and to teach the people (1:38). His ministry in Galilee involved "preaching in their synagogues and casting out demons" (1:39).

The number of characters who engage in proclamation is noteworthy. In fact, something of a chain of proclamation is set up at the beginning, with John the Baptist "proclaiming a baptism of repentance for the forgiveness of sins" (1:4) and promising that a greater one would follow him (1:7–8). After John's arrest, Jesus begins his own ministry by "proclaiming the gospel of God" (1:14). He, in turn, commissions the disciples to preach (3:14) and later sends them to proclaim "that people should repent" (6:12). The pattern established is that discipleship—following Jesus—involves proclamation. We see this illustrated when Jesus commands the Gerasene demoniac to go and tell people what the Lord had done for him. In obedience "he went away and began to proclaim in the Decapolis how much Jesus had done for him" (5:20).

7   So, e.g., Robert A. Guelich, *Mark 1–8:26*, WBC (Dallas: Word, 1989), 70.

8   So, e.g., Simon Gathercole, *The Preexistent Son: Recovering the Christologies of Matthew, Mark, and Luke* (Grand Rapids, MI: Eerdmans, 2006), 154–57.

9   R. T. France, *The Gospel of Mark: A Commentary on the Greek Text*, NIGTC (Grand Rapids, MI: Eerdmans, 2002), 113.

The expectation that discipleship involves proclamation is underlined in Jesus's discourse in 13:9–10. He expects that the disciples will "bear witness" before "governors and kings for my sake" (13:9) and that "the gospel must first be proclaimed to all nations" (13:10; cf. 14:9). The connection between discipleship and proclamation is also made in 8:34–35. Disciples are not just called to lose their lives for Jesus's sake but also for the gospel's sake.

But what of the commands to silence we noticed earlier? The consensus is that this silence motif has three aspects.[10] First, there was a strategic concern. A misconstrued claim to messiahship might have been seen as politically dangerous, provoking Roman intervention. Peter's identification of Jesus as the Messiah (8:29) is followed by his failure to understand the necessity of Jesus's death (8:32). A widespread expectation that Jesus would immediately institute a Psalm 2:9-type of kingship may have hindered his ministry. This perhaps explains why the Gerasene demoniac in Mark 5:19 is encouraged to speak about what Jesus has done for him. The likelihood of messianic fervor being stoked by the testimony of a Gentile in Gentile territory would have been low.

Second, Jesus's silence may have a Christological aspect. His desire to be hidden may suggest that he shaped his ministry after the servant of the Lord prophesied in Isaiah. Isaiah 49:2 speaks both of the servant's ability to speak—"[God] made my mouth like a sharp sword"—and of his hiddenness:

> in the shadow of his hand he hid me;
> he made me a polished arrow;
> in his quiver he hid me away.

Similarly in Isaiah 42:2, the servant is described as one who

> will not cry aloud or lift up his voice,
> or make it heard in the street.

---

10 The remainder of this section is a summary of James R. Edwards, *The Gospel according to Mark*, PNTC (Grand Rapids, MI: Eerdmans, 2002), 62–63.

Matthew uses this verse to explain Jesus's ministry (Matt. 12:19). Although Mark does not explicitly cite it, nevertheless the indications he gives point to the same understanding: Jesus's ministry is shaped by that of Isaiah's servant.

Finally, the command to silence may reflect the reality that Jesus and his mission could not be adequately understood before the cross and resurrection. This leads to a consideration of the fact that revelation is not a naturally occurring phenomenon.

The Secret Is Given

In addition to presenting revelation as written and proclaimed, Mark also shows that revelation can't be received by people without a prior work of God. We are introduced to this in Mark 4 when Jesus begins to teach in parables. The first parable (of the sower), combined with Jesus's explanation, teaches that revelation involves more than merely hearing God's word. The four soils represent four types of people who hear the word (4:15, 16, 18, 20). However, the word only produces lasting fruit in the "good soil," which represents those who "hear the word and accept it and bear fruit" (4:20). Though each person heard the word, only one type accepted it and bore fruit. The parable is less an *exhortation* to become good soil than an *explanation* of revelation, something on which Jesus expands in the aftermath of this first parable.

Parables were not invented by Jesus. The word *parabolē* in the Septuagint refers to a variety of modes of speaking (e.g., Num. 23:7; 2 Sam. 23:3). The basic definition is a "narrative or saying of varying length, designed to illustrate a truth especially through comparison or simile."[11] Although the word *parabolē* is not used in the account, the story that Nathan tells David in 2 Samuel 12:1–6 resembles the parables that Jesus tells. Furthermore, it is instructive that David doesn't grasp the meaning of the parable until Nathan interprets it for him: "You are the man!" (2 Sam. 12:7).

---

11   "Παραβολή," BDAG 759.

Jesus finishes this first parable with the words, "He who has ears to hear, let him hear" (Mark 4:9). When they are alone, the disciples question him about the parables. This includes not only the twelve but "those around him with the twelve" (4:10). People who *approach* Jesus and *ask* for an explanation receive it. Those in the crowd who turn away do not. Jesus tells this smaller group, "To you has been given the secret of the kingdom of God," in contrast to those "outside" for whom "everything is in parables" (4:11). We will consider the reason for this below (in Jesus's citation of Isa. 6:9–10), but for now note that Jesus relates to those inside and outside differently.

The insiders receive "the secret of the kingdom" (4:11). "Secret" is *mystērion* and is elsewhere translated "mystery" (e.g., Rom. 11:25, 16:25; Rev. 1:20). This word stands out in the LXX of Daniel 2–4 where God alone reveals mysteries to Daniel (e.g., Dan. 2:19; 2:28). There, when he appears before Nebuchadnezzar, Daniel insists that to explain dreams is impossible for human beings, but "there is a God in heaven who reveals mysteries" (Dan. 2:27–28). When Jesus tells the disciples that they have been "given the secret of the kingdom of God," he is indicating that *God* has revealed this mystery to them. This fits with Nebuchadnezzar's response in Daniel 2:47: "Truly, your God is God of gods and Lord of kings, and a revealer of mysteries, for you have been able to reveal this mystery." A mystery is "something 'given' rather than deciphered, with a view to that revelation being shared with others, which is essential to all its uses in the NT, including here in relation to parables."[12]

Many assume that Jesus told parables to make his teaching simpler and more accessible. However, the citation of Isaiah 6:9–10 in Mark 4:12 belies that assumption. Isaiah is commissioned by God to execute judgment on the people of Israel:

Make the heart of this people dull,
    and their ears heavy,
    and blind their eyes. (Isa. 6:10a)

---

12 France, *Mark*, 196.

His preaching is to be veiled precisely so that people won't

> see with their eyes,
>> and hear with their ears,
>> and understand with their hearts,
>> and turn and be healed. (Isa. 6:10b)

In citing this part of Isaiah, Jesus attributes the same effect to his parables. They serve as an instrument of judgment so that people

> may indeed see but not perceive,
>> and may indeed hear but not understand,
>> lest they should turn and be forgiven. (Mark 4:12)

It is not as if the parables are incomprehensible nonsense, leaving people scratching their heads as they wander away. The stories themselves make sense on a purely descriptive level. The parable of the sower is intelligible as a description of the experience of most farmers. However, to penetrate to the spiritual meaning and implication behind the parable requires that the hearer be given "the secret of the kingdom" (4:11).

Yet, as privileged as these insiders are, revelation does not stop at the level of Jesus's instruction of them. He gives a mild rebuke in 4:13 before he explains the parable: "Do you not understand this parable? How then will you not understand all the parables?" Yes, they are insiders, but the only difference between them and the outsiders is that they receive the explanation from Jesus. As the narrative continues, Mark focuses on the twelve whose inability to grasp what Jesus is teaching often makes them no different from outsiders.

Deaf Ears, Blind Eyes, Hard Hearts

Mark uses the sensory imagery of hearing and seeing as well as the bodily imagery of eyes, ears, and hearts to teach that revelation, to be complete, needs to be *received*. The reason for speaking in parables is, as we have seen, to keep outsiders out—so that

they may indeed see but not perceive,
    and may indeed hear but not understand,
lest they should turn and be forgiven. (4:12)

Their sight and hearing only operate at a surface level. The Greek is a little more unusual, using two different "seeing" words: "so that looking they may look [blepōsin] and not see [idōsin]." They see but do not really see.

Jesus rebukes the twelve for precisely this lack of understanding. In 7:18, when the disciples question him about his interaction with the Pharisees concerning the nature of ritual purity, he asks them if they are "also without understanding." In 8:18 following another misunderstanding of what Jesus was teaching, he asks the twelve, "Having eyes do you not see, and having ears do you not hear? And do you not remember?"

Eyes to See

The visual imagery of "eye" and "seeing" runs throughout the Gospel. Not only does Mark speak of people's perception or lack of it, he also applies seeing language to Jesus himself. Jesus models correct perception with the eyes. At his baptism as he comes out of the water, Mark tells us that "he saw" the heavens open and the Spirit descending (1:10). When a paralytic is brought to Jesus, Mark says that Jesus "saw" the faith of the friends carrying him (2:5). Jesus correctly perceives these spiritual realities.

Jesus's sight also connects to his pastoral care. He "saw" the great crowd "like sheep without a shepherd" (6:34), and he had compassion on them, teaching and feeding them (6:34–44). He "saw" the disciples struggling on the water before he walked on the sea to them (6:48). However, sight can also express his judgment. As Jesus discussed with members of the synagogue about whether it is appropriate to heal on the Sabbath, Mark tells us that "he looked around at them with anger, grieved at their hardness of heart" (3:5). Later he goes to "see" if a fig tree has any fruit on it, and when he finds none, he curses it (11:13–14).

Seeing language also appears when Jesus summons his disciples. The callings of Simon and Andrew (1:16), James and John (1:19), and Levi (2:14) are all preceded by Mark telling us that Jesus "saw" those he was going to call. An otherwise incidental detail, I think, is perhaps given more significance by the importance of seeing throughout the book. Similarly, when Jesus is informed that his mother and brothers are outside, he was "looking about" at those sitting around him and identified them as his family (3:34).

Jesus frequently calls for correct sight: "watch out [*orate*]; beware [*blepete*] of the leaven of the Pharisees and the leaven of Herod" (8:15; cf. 12:38). Later he warns the disciples, "See [*blepete*] that no one leads you astray" (13:5). The command to "watch [*blepete*]" (ESV: "be on guard") echoes throughout this chapter (13:9, 23, 33).

Throughout the Gospel, Mark narrates correct and incorrect perceptions of Jesus. He describes amazement when people see Jesus's miracles. When Jesus heals a paralytic, they respond, "we never saw anything like this!" (2:12). We are told that, "seeing him," Jairus fell at his feet (5:22). When he comes down the mountain "the crowd, when they saw him, were greatly amazed" and ran to greet him (9:15). Demon-possessed people, upon seeing Jesus, indicate that they know who he is. With the boy afflicted by a spirit, we read that "when the spirit saw him" it reacted by convulsing the boy, causing him to fall and foam at the mouth (9:20).

After the transfiguration when the disciples look around, they "no longer saw anyone with them but Jesus only" (9:8). The scribe whom Jesus says is "not far from the kingdom of God" (12:34) was described as "seeing that [Jesus] answered them well" (12:28). Correct sight is emphasized in the citation of Psalm 118:22–23 in Mark 12:10–11. The psalmist recognizes that exalting the rejected stone as the cornerstone is "the Lord's doing" and that "it is marvelous in our eyes" (12:11). Here is the essence of correct sight—recognizing the rejected stone as the cornerstone. The most dramatic example of correct perception, though, comes at Jesus's death when the centurion who "saw" how Jesus died, confessed him as the "Son of God" (15:39). This is a model example of someone recognizing the rejected stone as the cornerstone.

Yet, sometimes "seeing" leads to the wrong response. When the Gerasene demoniac "saw Jesus from afar, he ran and fell down before him"—an appropriate response (5:6). However, when this man was healed by Jesus, people heard about it and "came to see" what had happened. When they "saw the demon-possessed man" now sitting there healed and in his right mind, "they were afraid" (5:14–15). Furthermore, when those who "had seen" (5:16) the miracle told this new crowd what Jesus had done, they begged "Jesus to depart from their region" (5:17). When Jesus walked toward the disciples on the water, they "saw him walking on the sea" and "thought it was a ghost" (6:49). They "all saw him and were terrified" (6:50). Seeing Jesus and his miraculous activity, then, sometimes led to the inappropriate response of fear.

The eyes can, with the heart, be the source of sin. "Envy" in 7:22 is a translation of the Greek "evil eye." Jesus teaches that if your "eye causes you to sin," it is better to tear it out so that you can enter the kingdom of God (9:47). We also read of "accusatory seeing" where people see what Jesus is doing and perceive it negatively. When the Pharisees "saw that he was eating with sinners and tax collectors," they question his disciples about it (2:16). Later they "saw that some of his disciples ate" with unwashed hands (7:2).

Thus, the act of seeing can lead to appropriate or inappropriate responses to Jesus. Even the disciples do not innately make correct perceptions regarding Jesus. There may be an allusion to this negative spiritual state in the garden of Gethsemane when the disciples are unable to stay awake because "their eyes were very heavy" (14:40).

How does correct perception come about? Jesus certainly anticipates that the disciples will "see" correctly in the future. He warns that, when they "see the abomination of desolation" standing where it should not, they are to flee (13:14). Similarly, when they "see these things taking place," they know that "he is near" (13:29). In the future, the disciples *will* heed the warnings of Jesus to "see" correctly. This contrasts with the time of his earthly ministry when he rebukes them in the strongest way possible: "Do you not yet perceive or understand? Are your hearts hardened? Having eyes do you not see, and having ears do you not hear?" (8:17–18). What changes their imperception in Mark 8 to the future perception described in Mark 13? Before I address that question, we need to consider the related imagery of hearing.

Ears to Hear

Hearing and seeing combine in 4:24. The English "pay attention to what you hear" is a good translation, but the Greek suggests a tighter relationship between seeing and hearing: "watch [or see] what you hear [*blepete ti akouete*]." The theme of ears/hearing parallels that of eyes/seeing and is equally developed in Mark. Jesus frequently exhorts people to listen correctly: "He who has ears to hear, let him hear" (4:9 cf. 4:23; 7:14). At the transfiguration the disciples are commanded by God to "listen to" Jesus (9:7). The obvious Old Testament background is Moses's promise in Deuteronomy 18:15: "The LORD your God will raise up for you a prophet like me from among you, from your brothers—it is to him you shall listen."

Just as crowds respond with amazement to what they see, they also marvel at what they hear. For example, "When the great crowd heard all that he was doing, they came to him" (3:8 cf. 6:55). Others who had heard of his miracles approach Jesus for their own healing, such as the woman subject to bleeding in 5:27 and the Gentile woman with a demon-possessed daughter in 7:25. The crowds are astonished that Jesus "even makes the deaf hear and the mute speak" (7:37). Those witnessing him debating with the Jewish leaders "heard him gladly" (12:37). When Bartimaeus "heard" that Jesus was passing by, he cried out to him for mercy (10:47).

The parable of the sower emphasizes the need to hear correctly as it recounts four different types of people, each of whom is said to "hear" (4:15, 16, 18, 20), but only the people represented by the good soil "hear the word and accept it and bear fruit" (4:20). True hearing, then, leads to long-lasting fruitfulness. Jesus's role as a teacher is complemented by the emphasis on listening. Jesus himself warned people to "pay attention to what you hear" (4:24).

However, just as one can fail to see properly, one can also mishear. At one point such a large crowd gathers around Jesus that he and his disciples "could not even eat" (Mark 3:20). Mark tells us that "when his family heard it," they went to seize him, thinking that he was "out of his mind" (3:21). When the disciples are sent out on mission, Jesus tells them to shake the dust off their feet if any place "will not listen to you" (6:11). When the chief priests and scribes hear about Jesus overturning the money changers and quoting Scripture to justify his actions, they renew their plans to kill him (11:18). When Jesus cries out in the words of Psalm 22:1, the bystanders mishear and think that he is calling Elijah (15:35).

Hearts to Understand

Seeing and hearing are more than physical activities in Mark's Gospel. True sight and hearing must lead to genuine understanding, something that Jesus underlines, for example, when he exhorts people, "Hear me, all of you, and understand" (7:14). It is not enough to simply listen to him; they need to understand as well (cf. 8:21, "Do you not yet understand?"). As well as being connected to the ears and eyes, understanding is also a function of the heart. The disciples' failure to "understand about the loaves" is an indication that "their hearts were hardened" (6:52). This connection is repeated in Jesus's rebuke to them in 8:17 when he asks, "Do you not yet perceive or understand? Are your hearts hardened?" Failure to understand is not just an indication of blind eyes and deaf ears but of a hard heart.

Hardness of heart leads the Pharisees to judge Jesus (2:6) and shows itself in their unwillingness to see human suffering relieved on the Sabbath (3:5). A heart that "is far from" God is seen in mere lip service (7:6) and disobedience to his commands (7:8). The heart is the place from which sin comes and renders a person unclean (7:21–23). In contrast, a person with genuine faith will "not doubt in his heart" (11:23). The greatest commandment is to "love the Lord your God with all your heart" (12:30). A soft heart, in other words, will be seen in its faith, love, and obedience.

How is a person restored to correct sight, right hearing, and a soft heart? The two most unusual miracles in the Gospel—the healing of the deaf man (7:31–37) and the healing of the blind man (8:22–26)—show that Jesus's intervention restores this sight and hearing.

In 7:31–37 a man is brought to Jesus who is "deaf and had a speech impediment" (7:32). The crowd begs Jesus to heal him, which he proceeds to do, but in a more unusual manner than his other miracles. Jesus removes the man from the crowd and "put his fingers into his ears, and after spitting touched his tongue" (7:33). He then looks to heaven, sighs, and says (in Aramaic), "Ephphatha," which means, "Be opened" (7:34). The man's ears are opened, and he can hear and speak.

The healing of the blind man in 8:22–26 has a number of similarities (e.g., the use of saliva[13]) and is equally strange but for different reasons. Here Jesus heals the man in two stages. Again, he spits and this time touches the man's eyes. The man can now see, but as he looks, he says, "I see people, but they look like trees, walking" (8:24). Jesus again touches the man's eyes, and this time his sight is fully restored.

Why are these two healings marked by such unusual features? It seems that they are symbolic of the disciples' need. The two-stage healing of the blind man corresponds to Peter's two-stage understanding of Jesus—that is, Peter grasps Jesus's identity as the Christ (8:29) but then promptly reveals an ongoing (partial) blindness by failing to understand the necessity of Jesus's death. Only after the resurrection will Peter and the other disciples understand more fully who Jesus is and why he came. In 8:18 Jesus rebuked the disciples' inability to see or hear, thus establishing this metaphorical understanding for blindness and deafness.

Although sometimes this metaphorical interpretation can be adopted a little too simplistically, it does seem to fit with Mark's agenda. Robert Stein objects to the metaphorical interpretation, arguing that it is both very subtle and relies on the fact that the disciples only came to

13 See Robert H. Stein (*Mark*, BECNT [Grand Rapids, MI: Baker Academic, 2008], 388) for more parallels between the two healings.

a full understanding post-resurrection—something not located within the Gospel.[14] On the first objection, we have already seen that Mark is a subtle, elusive writer. On the second, I have argued that Mark writes to an audience with some knowledge of the gospel already and an awareness of the disciples and their proclamation of the gospel. Furthermore, Mark makes clear that the disciples will ultimately understand. Jesus speaks of a time when they will "stand before governors and kings for my sake, to bear witness" (13:9) and the Holy Spirit will provide them the words to say (13:11).[15]

This connection of hearing and seeing suggests that when they are restored, the heart will follow. A hard heart fails to understand (8:17); a restored heart corresponds to correct sight and hearing. The person who hears and perceives correctly will have a genuine heart that loves God (12:30), does not doubt (11:23), and obeys his commands (7:8).

When we consider salvation in Mark's Gospel in the next chapter, we will see that it includes forgiveness. Thus, salvation is more than revelation; nevertheless, revelation is critical. Jesus needs to open our eyes and ears so that we perceive him correctly. Mark's understanding of the connection between the heart, spiritual perception, and salvation has echoes in Isaiah, which speaks of the dangerous state of idolaters: "They know not, nor do they discern," and they are in this predicament because God "has shut their eyes, so that they cannot see, and their hearts, so that they cannot understand" (Isa. 44:18). The parallels with Mark are strong—even though idolatry is not prominent in this Gospel. Critically, Isaiah then connects this spiritual blindness and hardheartedness with an inability to save oneself: "A deluded heart has led him astray, and he cannot deliver himself or say, 'Is there not a lie in my right hand?'" (Isa. 44:20). Blindness and deluded hearts mean that people cannot deliver themselves but need God's intervention—which Isaiah affirms two verses later with God's words:

14   Stein, *Mark*, 388.
15   A point made in Adela Yarbro Collins, *Mark: A Commentary on the Gospel of Mark*, Hermeneia (Minneapolis: Fortress, 2007), 395.

I have blotted out your transgressions like a cloud
   and your sins like mist;
return to me, for I have redeemed you. (Isa. 44:22)

The universal plight is a corrupt heart from which sin flows (Mark 7:21–23). A corrupt heart cannot see or understand. Right perception (seeing and hearing) can only be restored by Jesus's intervention.

Conclusion

Mark offers a sophisticated theology of revelation. We have the objective revelation of the Old Testament Scriptures and the proclamation of the gospel by John, Jesus, and the disciples. On one level revelation is open to all—the gospel is publicly proclaimed and Jesus freely teaches all who will listen. However, it is only those who approach Jesus and remain with him who receive the "secret of the kingdom" (4:11).

As readers of Mark's Gospel, we are in the privileged position of the insider. For example, when we read Jesus's explanation of the parable of the sower (4:13–20), we are in the same position as the disciples who ask and receive the "secret of the kingdom" (4:10–11). However, this does not allow us to remain in a neutral stance toward the words written in the Gospel. Jesus's explanation of the parable of the sower was an invitation for people to listen carefully. The secrets are meant to come to light (4:22); this means that "if anyone has ears to hear, let him hear" (4:23). A generous listening to Jesus will be rewarded (4:24–25). This applies to readers of Mark's Gospel as much as it did to Jesus's listeners.

Revelation ultimately must be received, but Mark shows that this is beyond natural capability. Even the disciples who stand in the privileged position of insiders fail to see, to hear, and to perceive. Their hearts are hardened. Mark presents the disciples only coming to partial understanding within the narrative (e.g., 8:29, 31–33) but assumes they will fully understand later when they faithfully proclaim the gospel, with the Holy Spirit's prompting, to the world (13:9–12).

What makes the difference? Jesus's healing. He opens blind eyes (8:22–26) and deaf ears (7:31–35). The unusual nature of both of these healings highlights their significance. In chapter 4, we will see how Mark connects physical healing and spiritual salvation. In this chapter we have seen him connect eyes, ears, and hearts. To heal ears and eyes symbolizes the healing of the heart—the center of human corruption (7:20–23).

Mark's theology of revelation corresponds closely to what we find in Paul—particularly 1 Corinthians. Paul reflects on his own preaching and how his message was simply "Jesus Christ and him crucified" (1 Cor. 2:2). This is wisdom, though not the wisdom of the world but "a secret and hidden wisdom of God" (1 Cor. 2:7). It is only by the Spirit "that we might understand the things freely given us by God" (1 Cor. 2:12). However, the "natural person does not accept the things of the Spirit of God, for they are folly to him, and he is not able to understand them because they are spiritually discerned" (1 Cor. 2:14). In different words, then, Paul's theology of revelation lines up with that of Mark. The latter does not refer to the Holy Spirit except in a few places (Mark 1:8, 10, 12; 3:29; 12:36; 13:11) and does not tie his role closely to revelation. However, both Mark and Paul agree that correct reception of revelation is *naturally* impossible. While Paul emphasizes the role of the Spirit, Mark emphasizes the role of Christ in granting this supernatural revelation. These are complementary ideas that can be seen when Paul defines the "spiritual person" as the person who has the "mind of Christ" (1 Cor. 2:15–16).

The Kingdom of God Is at Hand

Jesus and the New Creation

COMPARE THE BEGINNINGS of the Gospels. Matthew provides a genealogy situating Jesus in the history of Israel followed by a birth narrative. Luke has a longer birth narrative and then a genealogy that traces Jesus back to Adam. John refers to Jesus's eternal presence with God. Mark, in contrast, has Jesus burst onto the scene seemingly from nowhere. John the Baptist announces his arrival, and then we are simply told that "in those days Jesus came from Nazareth of Galilee" (Mark 1:9).

But if Jesus seems to come from nowhere, his message has a history. The Isaiah quotation in Mark 1:2–3 establishes the continuity with the Old Testament, as do his first words: "The time is fulfilled, and the kingdom of God is at hand" (1:15). The theme of the kingdom of God situates Jesus in the flow of redemptive history.

The announcement of the kingdom gives way to specific teachings on the kingdom throughout the Gospel (particularly through the parables) together with demonstrations of the kingdom's inbreaking in Jesus's healings, encounters with demons, and other miracles. We will see that the kingdom of God is not an abstract reality (e.g., a vague idea of "the reign of God") but is tied to two concrete realities—Jesus Christ and the new creation.

The Time Is Fulfilled: The Kingdom Is at Hand

To grasp Jesus's words, "the kingdom of God is at hand," we need to first understand what he means by "the time is fulfilled" (*peplērōtai ho kairos*). The word *kairos* in Mark can refer to both a *span of time* (e.g., 10:30, where it parallels "age" [*aiōnios*]; 11:13, rendered as "season") or *a particular, appointed time* (e.g., 13:33, "you do not know when the *kairos* will come"). So, in 1:15, is Jesus saying that "the span of time has passed" or "the decisive moment has arrived"?

Although Eckhard Schnabel suggests that *both* are in view,[1] most commentators think that Jesus means a "decisive time has arrived."[2] Admittedly the difference is subtle, but the meaning of the verb "fulfill" (*plēroō*) and its use here in the perfect passive push us toward the latter view. This perfect passive is probably best understood as stressing the present "state" of fulfilment, which is reflected in most translations: "The time is fulfilled" (rather than "the time has been fulfilled").[3] In other words, the emphasis is on the present: *this* is the time of fulfillment.

The fact that Jesus's first words are "the kingdom of God is at hand" is also significant, for it shows how he summarizes the entire period of expectation. He does not say "the exile is over" or even "salvation has come"—although both of these are connected to the kingdom—but "the kingdom of God is at hand."

The expression "kingdom of God" does not occur in the Old Testament. However, God is frequently presented as a king. "The LORD became king in Jeshurun" at Sinai (Deut. 33:5).[4] When Israel asks Samuel for a king, God reflects that "they have rejected me from being king over them" (1 Sam. 8:7). Declaring that he will establish David's line, God promises to confirm David's offspring "in my house

---

1   Eckhard J. Schnabel, *Mark: An Introduction and Commentary*, TNTC (Downers Grove, IL: IVP Academic, 2017), 51.

2   James R. Edwards, *The Gospel according to Mark*, PNTC (Grand Rapids, MI: Eerdmans, 2002), 47; Robert A. Guelich, *Mark 1–8:26*, WBC (Dallas: Word, 1989), 43.

3   I am following the work of Robert Crellin. For a summary, see Robert Crellin, "The Greek Perfect Active System: 200 BC – AD 150," *TynBul* 64, no. 1 (2013): 157–60. He does discuss passive examples in this article.

4   Jeshurun is a poetic name for Israel (cf. Isa. 44:2).

and in my kingdom forever" (1 Chron. 17:14). The Psalms perhaps reflect on God's kingship the most. This is striking because this book articulates the experiences of the human kings (predominantly David) whom God has appointed over the people. The Psalms ground David's kingship in the more fundamental reality of God's reign. They reflect on the eternal nature of God's kingdom[5] and the supremacy of his kingship.[6]

Jesus's opening words suggest that God's kingdom is a dynamic reality. He says that the kingdom of God "is at hand" or "has drawn near"—using another perfect tense verb, *ēngiken*. This verb appears in the active voice, with the sense that the kingdom is on the cusp of dawning—indeed in some sense is already here. This tension between what has been called the "now" and the "not yet" of the kingdom runs throughout the New Testament and no less in Mark's Gospel. This ambiguity exists because "for Mark and his readers, the kingdom is directly related to Jesus himself. The king is present so the kingdom is near. It has drawn near spatially in Jesus's person and temporally in the actions of God to achieve eschatological salvation."[7] As R. T. France notes, the "main point of Mark 1:15 is not the precise timescale, but the fact that it is *in the coming of Jesus* that we are to see God's revolution taking place. Indeed, it is *in Jesus* that we are to see God coming as king."[8]

In the rest of this chapter, we will look at the kingdom in Mark's Gospel through two lenses. First, we will examine direct references to the kingdom either in the teaching of Jesus or in the narrative itself ("the kingdom taught"). Second, we will explore how the kingdom was demonstrated or experienced through Jesus's ministry ("the kingdom experienced").

---

5 For example, "your throne, O God, is forever and ever" (Ps. 45:6); "your kingdom is an everlasting kingdom" (Ps. 145:13; cf. Pss. 10:16; 29:10).

6 For example, "For the Lord is a great God, and a great King above all gods" (Ps. 95:3; cf. Pss. 47:2; 103:19).

7 Mark L. Strauss, *Mark*, ZECNT (Grand Rapids, MI: Zondervan Academic, 2014), 82.

8 R. T. France, *Divine Government: God's Kingship in the Gospel of Mark* (London: SPCK, 1990), 24–25 (emphasis in original).

The Kingdom Taught

In Mark 4 we have some of Jesus's most direct teaching on the kingdom. In 4:11 he explains his practice of teaching in parables to the disciples because to them "has been given the secret of the kingdom of God, but for those outside everything is in parables." He follows this explanation (in response to the parable of the sower) with the parable of the growing seed (4:26–29) where he makes a comparison: "The kingdom of God is as if a man should scatter seed on the ground," and it grows in a way that "he knows not how" (4:26–27). The point is that the grain grows unnoticed, without the farmer's intervention. As Paul puts it in 1 Corinthians 3:7, God "gives the growth."

Similarly, Jesus compares the kingdom to a mustard seed that, though the smallest known seed at the time, grows to become "larger than all the garden plants" (Mark 4:32). To summarize, Jesus teaches that the kingdom of God would grow extensively (parable of the mustard seed) and without the need for human aid (parable of the growing seed). However, the parable of the sower and Jesus's explanation of it suggest that not everyone belongs to the kingdom. Some remain outside.

The next reference to the kingdom of God comes just before the transfiguration of Jesus (9:1), which we will consider in the section on the transfiguration below. But in between we have the gruesome account of John the Baptist's death at the hands of Herod (6:14–29). Frequently labeled a king (6:14, 22, 25, 26, 27), Herod offers up to half of his kingdom to Herodias's daughter because her dancing pleased him (6:23). The juxtaposition of this weak, despotic king with Jesus, the good shepherd who cares for his flock by teaching and feeding them (6:30–44), is striking.

The second half of the Gospel, following Peter's confession (8:27–30), stresses the need to "enter" the kingdom of God. Entering is so important that it is better "to enter the kingdom of God with one eye than with two eyes to be thrown into hell" (9:47). To enter the kingdom of God, one must receive it "like a child," for "to such belongs the kingdom of God" (10:14–15). However, entering the kingdom is not easy. In fact, "it is easier for a camel to go through the eye of a needle than for a rich person to enter the kingdom of God" (10:25). But this difficulty is not reserved for the wealthy. Jesus expands the problem more universally when he states, "How difficult it is to enter the kingdom of God!" (10:24). In this context "to enter the kingdom" equates with "to inherit eternal life" (10:17). Thus, "anything that causes disciples to forget their poverty and childlikeness before God and that prevents them from following Jesus Christ—this, too, is a camel before the eye of a needle."[9] Perhaps because they understand wealth as a sign of God's blessing,[10] the disciples are "exceedingly astonished" at this teaching and ask Jesus, "Then who can be saved?" (10:26). Jesus replies that this is impossible—no human being whether rich or poor can be saved. Nevertheless, "with God" it is possible (10:27). That is, from "the perspective of the kingdom of God, who is the Creator and who can do everything (9:23), the salvation of the rich and indeed of any human being becomes a possibility."[11] To a scribe who understood that loving God and loving neighbor were the most important aspects of the law, Jesus declares that he is "not far from the kingdom of God" (12:34).

In the ensuing discussion, Peter remarks that he and his companions have "left everything and followed" Jesus (10:28). Jesus affirms that those who have done so will receive "a hundredfold *now in this time*" (i.e., a Christian family *and* persecutions) "and *in the age to come* eternal life" (10:30). The fact of blessing in the present and in the future reflects the temporal ambiguity of the kingdom. Jesus's concluding words that "many who are first will be last, and the last first" (10:31) teaches "the great eschatological reversal that is characteristic of the present and the future appearance of the kingdom of God."[12] Not the rich but the persecuted followers of Jesus receive God's kingdom blessing.[13]

As we approach the end of Mark's Gospel, the future kingdom dominates. Jesus enters Jerusalem with the crowd's acclamation: "Blessed is

9 Edwards, *Mark*, 314.
10 Strauss (*Mark*, 443) notes Prov. 10:22: "The blessing of the LORD makes rich."
11 Schnabel, *Mark*, 244.
12 Strauss, *Mark*, 446.
13 Strauss, *Mark*, 446.

the *coming* kingdom of our father David!" (11:10). At the Last Supper, Jesus tells his disciples that he will forgo wine until he will "drink it new in the kingdom of God" (14:25). The final reference to the kingdom in the book follows Jesus's death. Joseph of Arimathea, who asks Pilate for Jesus's body, is described as "looking for the kingdom of God" (15:43). However, as the cross approaches, these future references are also interwoven with markers to Jesus's present kingship. The sign above the cross identifies Jesus as "the King of the Jews" (15:26). The chief priests and scribes mock that "the Christ, the King of Israel" should come down from the cross so that they might "see and believe" (15:32).

Our brief survey shows that the kingdom is dynamic—it draws near (1:15), grows (4:26–30), comes with power (9:1; cf. 11:10; see the section on the transfiguration below), can be received (10:15), and can be waited for (15:43). Yet, it is also conceived of spatially so that it can be entered (9:47; 10:23). A person can be "in" the kingdom (14:25) or "outside" (4:11). It can be conceived of in terms of the distance from a person (cf. 12:34, "you are not far from the kingdom of God"). As we approach the end of the Gospel the references to kingdom fall away and the references to Jesus as King increase.

The Kingdom Experienced

Mark's Gospel also teaches us about the kingdom by showing the effect of Jesus's coming into the world. In this section I will examine three groups of events: his battle with the kingdom of Satan, his healings, and the transfiguration. The latter in particular, we will see, shows that for Mark the kingdom is a new-creation reality.

The Clash of Kingdoms

Following Jesus's baptism and the Spirit's anointing, the Spirit immediately drove Jesus into the wilderness where Satan tempted him for forty days. Mark tells us that he was with the wild animals and that the angels ministered to him (1:12–13). This is a much shorter account than in either Matthew (Matt. 4:1–11) or Luke (Luke 4:1–13); however, the event is nevertheless significant within Mark's Gospel. It underlines that Jesus's life and ministry unfolds against the backdrop of cosmic conflict.[14] On one side stands Jesus (and the angels with God; cf. Mark 13:32); on the other side stands Satan (and his demons).

In Jesus's debate with the Jerusalem scribes in Mark 3, the conflict comes into focus—it is a clash of kingdoms. The scribes accuse Jesus of casting out demons "by the prince of demons" and being "possessed by Beelzebul" (3:22). Jesus points out the absurdity of this charge: it would suggest that Satan expels himself (3:23). He then declares the principle: "If a kingdom is divided against itself, that kingdom cannot stand" (3:24). Jesus pushes the application beyond kingdoms: "If a house is divided against itself, that house will not be able to stand. And if Satan has risen up against himself and is divided, he cannot stand, but is coming to an end" (3:25–26). The logical impossibility of Satan exorcising Satan exposes the absurdity of the scribes' accusation. What then does explain Jesus's ability to drive out demons? Extending the house imagery, Jesus states, "No one can enter a strong man's house and plunder his goods, unless he first binds the strong man. Then indeed he may plunder his house" (3:27).

When does Jesus bind and plunder the strong man? Does he first bind him during the temptation and then plunder him throughout the Gospel as he drives out demons?[15] Or does the binding of the strong man evoke Isaiah 53:12?

He shall divide the spoil with the strong,
> because he poured out his soul to death
and was numbered with the transgressors.

Understood this way, the binding could refer to Jesus's death and resurrection, and the subsequent plundering to the growth of the church.[16]

---

14 Schnabel, *Mark*, 47.

15 The argument of Adela Yarbro Collins, *Mark: A Commentary on the Gospel of Mark*, Hermeneia (Minneapolis: Fortress, 2007), 233.

16 Rikk E. Watts, "Mark," in *Commentary on the New Testament Use of the Old Testament*, ed. G. K. Beale and D. A. Carson (Grand Rapids, MI: Baker Academic, 2007), 294.

On balance, we probably should not press the logic of Mark 3:27 so as to suggest that the binding is a once-and-for-all action. Rather, we should understand that "each individual confrontation with Satan (in the person of one of the possessing demons who are under his control) will involve a 'power encounter', in which Jesus must assert his superior authority."[17]

Throughout Mark's Gospel, Jesus performs a number of exorcisms. The first occurs in Mark 1 as Jesus teaches in a synagogue where he encounters a demon possessed man "with" (*en*) an unclean spirit (1:23). Joel Marcus pinpoints the horror of the man's experience. The Greek preposition *en* suggests that he is "in" an impure spirit. If the *en* is locative, it indicates that the man is "enclosed by that which contaminates him"—a "horrifying" image,[18] which underlines the liberating power (and compassion) of Jesus.

The man cries out, "What have you to do with us, Jesus of Nazareth? Have you come to destroy us? I know who you are—the Holy One of God" (1:24). Jesus rebukes the man, commanding him to be silent and the demon to leave him. The spirit convulses the man, cries out, and then departs (1:25–26). The response of the people who witness this event is instructive. They are amazed and "questioned among themselves" before concluding that this is a "new teaching with authority," shown in the fact that Jesus "commands even the unclean spirits, and they obey him" (1:27). His ability to drive out demons, then, is understood as proof of the authority of his teaching.

This strength, power, and authority is demonstrated throughout the rest of the Gospel in Jesus's encounters with demon-possessed people, perhaps most dramatically in 5:1–20. Jesus arrives in the country of the Gerasenes by crossing the sea (5:1), perhaps a pointer to the cosmic conflict to follow.[19]

---

17 R. T. France, *The Gospel of Mark: A Commentary on the Greek Text*, NIGTC (Grand Rapids, MI: Eerdmans, 2002), 174.

18 Joel Marcus, *Mark 8–16: A New Translation with Introduction and Commentary*, AB (New Haven, CT: Yale University Press, 2009), 192. Marcus further comments, "The man's personality has been so usurped by the demon that the demon has, as it were, swallowed him up. The fusion of the man's identity with that of the demon is underlined by the grammar of the passage."

19 The sea is sometimes associated with cosmic conflict in Scripture. See, e.g., Job 7:12; Dan. 7:2–3; Hab. 3:15.

He encounters a man with an unclean spirit who dwells in the tombs (5:2). Mark then repeats the fact that the man lived among the tombs—underlining his inhabiting the realm of the dead[20]—and tells us that he could not be bound with chains for he had often broken his shackles (5:3–4). Mark emphasizes his tragic existence: "Night and day among the tombs and on the mountains he was always crying out and cutting himself with stones" (5:5). The man epitomizes life under Satan's dominion and the inability of humanity to escape from this control. However, upon seeing Jesus, the man "ran and fell down before him" (5:6). The power of Jesus sharply contrasts with the inability of any other human being to control this man. The demon is actually a "legion" of demons (5:9, 15), an indicator that "Jesus encounters not just one demon, but the kingdom of Satan."[21] Again by his mere spoken words, Jesus is able to drive out these demons and restore this man to "his right mind" (5:15).

Healings

Isaiah anticipates that healing proves the presence of the Lord "our king" (Isa. 33:22). Where he reigns,

> No inhabitant will say, "I am sick";
>> the people who dwell there will be forgiven their iniquity. (Isa. 33:24)

> The eyes of the blind shall be opened,
>> and the ears of the deaf unstopped;
> Then shall the lame man leap like a deer,
>> and the tongue of the mute sing for joy. (Isa. 35:5–6; cf. 29:18)

The Lord will send his servant

> to open the eyes that are blind,
> to bring out the prisoners from the dungeon,
>> from the prison those who sit in darkness. (Isa. 42:7)

---

20 Peter G. Bolt, *The Cross from a Distance: Atonement in Mark's Gospel*, NSBT (Downers Grove, IL: IVP Acadamic, 2004), 38.

21 Schnabel, *Mark*, 119.

Although the shortest Gospel, Mark recounts several healings that point to the fact that the kingdom of God has drawn near with Jesus's coming. Jesus heals "many who were sick with various diseases" (Mark 1:34), including a man with a skin disease that excluded him from the community (1:40–44). The healings of a paralytic (2:1–10) and of a man with a withered hand (3:1–6) are two events that bring Jesus into sharp conflict with the Jewish leadership. In 5:21–43 he heals a woman with a chronic discharge of blood and raises a synagogue ruler's daughter from death. In his hometown of Nazareth where people took offense at this local boy (6:3), Jesus still "laid hands on a few sick people and healed them" (6:5). In Gentile Gennesaret, even those who touched the fringe of his garment became well (6:56).

Mark 7–10 recalls a series of particularly significant healings that, while not more spectacular than raising a girl from the dead, are more biblically "marked"—that is, they point to the presence of the kingdom of God in a particularly resonant way. Jesus heals a deaf man in 7:31–37 and a man born blind in 8:22–26. Both healings (as I argued in chapter 2) are marked by their unusual features (with Jesus touching both men), highlighting their significance. They also indicate the powerful presence of the kingdom. In 7:37 the crowd is astonished because Jesus "makes the deaf hear and the mute speak." The use of the word for "mute" (*mogilalos*) in 7:32 (ESV: "had a speech impediment") is found only here and in LXX Isaiah 35:6 (quoted above). These healings thus seem to allude to Isaiah with its promise that when the Lord appears,

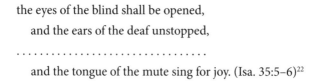

> the eyes of the blind shall be opened,
>   and the ears of the deaf unstopped,
> . . . .
>   and the tongue of the mute sing for joy. (Isa. 35:5–6)[22]

This pairing of deaf and blind healings is repeated on the other side of Peter's confession (8:29) in the healing of the boy with the deaf and

---

22 So Robert H. Stein, *Mark*, BECNT (Grand Rapids, MI: Baker Academic, 2008), 362.

mute spirit (9:14–28; which could also be considered an exorcism) and the healing of blind Bartimaeus (10:46–52).

One of Jesus's healings is worthy of clarification: the man with a skin disease in 1:40–45. Every English Bible version (that I have consulted at least) describes the man as "a leper," but the man *did not* have leprosy. The confusion is understandable since the underlying Greek word is *lepros* and he is said to suffer from *lepra*. However, the modern disease we call *leprosy*—that is, Hansen's disease—differs from the condition marked by *lepra*. Hansen's disease, if left untreated, can lead to paralysis and loss of body parts. Thankfully, it can be treated with medication and so is dying out.[23] The misassociation of what we know as Hansen's disease with the Greek term *lepra* stems from the eighth or ninth century.[24] In the Bible, *lepra* covered a range of conditions, not all of which were *medically* significant (the sorts of conditions that today might be treated with anti-fungal medication). The fact that Leviticus legislated for *lepra* spreading to a garment or a house (Lev. 13:47–59; 14:33–57) further shows that it is not the same as modern leprosy, which cannot infect inanimate objects.[25] Hansen's disease existed in the Mediterranean world but was known from around 200 BC as *elephantiasis*.[26]

If *lepra* was not as *medically* severe as Hansen's disease, it was nevertheless *ritually* significant. Healing someone with *lepra* was "comparable to raising the dead."[27] Notice the reaction of the king of Israel when the king of Syria writes asking him to cure his servant Naaman from *lepra* (the LXX rendering for the Hebrew *tsarat*): "Am I God, to kill and to make alive, that this man sends word to me to cure a man of his leprosy?" (2 Kings 5:7). Or Aaron's appeal to Moses to intercede

---

23 Most occurrences today are in India. I have visited the last leper colony in Europe, which is in Tichileşti in Romania. At the time of writing, it has nine inhabitants.

24 See Matthew Thiessen, *Jesus and the Forces of Death: The Gospels' Portrayal of Ritual Impurity Within First-Century Judaism* (Grand Rapids, MI: Baker Academic, 2021), 49.

25 Thiessen, *Jesus and the Forces of Death*, 46.

26 Thiessen, *Jesus and the Forces of Death*, 45–46.

27 Schnabel, *Mark*, 62.

for their sister Miriam when she was afflicted with *lepra*: "Let her not be as one dead" (Num. 12:12).[28]

Interestingly, whereas a word from Jesus can drive out demons, Jesus tends to touch those who have an illness or disease (though cf. Mark 2:10). For example, when Simon's mother-in-law is sick with a fever, Jesus "took her by the hand and lifted her up, and the fever left her" (1:31). Particularly significant is Jesus's touching of the man with *lepra*. The impurity does not flow from the man to Jesus; instead purity flows from Jesus to the man so that the *lepra* "left him, and he was made clean" (1:42). The same movement of purity *from* Jesus is seen with the bleeding woman (5:25–34) and Jairus's daughter (5:35–43), both of whom Jesus touches despite their ritual impurity.

The miracles, particularly the healings, point to the new-creation reality of the kingdom. They point forward to the time when the kingdom will be fully present, a time when creation will be renewed and there will be no more sickness or death.

Transfiguration

After Peter's confession and subsequent failure to understand the necessity of Jesus's death, Jesus announces, "There are some standing here who will not taste death until they see the kingdom of God after it has come with power" (9:1). Many think that Jesus here predicts his return ("the kingdom of God after it has come in power") before the death of the disciples (and others in the crowd; see 8:34).[29] Various possibilities are offered in the commentaries, but given that the pronouncement immediately precedes the transfiguration (in all three Synoptics), this event is the most likely fulfilment of Jesus's saying.

The narrative is straightforward. Jesus takes Peter, James, and John "up a high mountain" and is then "transfigured before them, and his

---

28 Thiessen, *Jesus and the Forces of Death*, 51.
29 Schnabel, *Mark*, 206. Schnabel provides a survey of the possible explanations for Jesus's reference to the coming of the kingdom, including (among others): Jesus was incorrect; the destruction of Jerusalem; the death and resurrection of Jesus.

clothes became radiant, intensely white, as no one on earth could bleach them" (9:2–3). Elijah and Moses appear and converse with Jesus. Peter, lost for words and "terrified," responds to what he sees by asking Jesus if he can build three tents: one each for Jesus, Moses, and Elijah (9:5–6). A cloud overshadows them and a voice from the cloud says, "This is my beloved Son; listen to him" (9:7). Then the disciples look around and see only Jesus.

Three aspects of this event contribute to our picture of Jesus: the *transfiguration* of Jesus himself, the presence of Moses and Elijah, and the voice from heaven. First, we observe that Jesus himself is transformed (i.e., not merely his clothes).[30] The question to ask is whether the light that Jesus radiates is his own divine glory or is *bestowed* on him. Kirk suggests that Jesus's divine identity is not being stressed since in this scene "there is neither application of the divine name, nor affirmation of a place in creation or rule over the cosmos, nor does Jesus receive worship."[31]

A number of Old Testament texts clarify the significance of Jesus's transfiguration. Daniel depicts the "Ancient of Days":

his clothing was white as snow,
    and the hair of his head like pure wool;
his throne was fiery flames;
    its wheels were burning fire. (Dan. 7:9; cf. the description of
        Jesus in Rev. 1:13–16)

The psalmist similarly describes God:

You are clothed with splendor and majesty,
    covering yourself with light as with a garment. (Ps. 104:1–2)[32]

---

30 See Simon Gathercole, *The Preexistent Son: Recovering the Christologies of Matthew, Mark, and Luke* (Grand Rapids, MI: Eerdmans, 2006), 49.

31 J. R. Daniel Kirk, *A Man Attested by God: The Human Jesus of the Synoptic Gospels* (Grand Rapids, MI: Eerdmans, 2016), 18.

32 Both texts are cited by Schnabel, *Mark*, 209.

Although neither of these exactly matches Mark's description of Jesus, the glorious imagery in Mark recalls these Old Testament texts, and thus God is "revealing the divine glory of Jesus."[33]

Stein attempts a more precise explanation of Jesus's transformation. Rather than recounting Jesus's preincarnate glory breaking through, Mark provides "a proleptic glimpse of the glory of the Son of Man / Son of God in his future coming (8:38), when the kingdom comes in power (9:1)."[34] However, one can overplay the distinction between Jesus's divine and human glory. Later in the New Testament, Jesus is said to reveal God because "he is the image of the invisible God, the firstborn of all creation" (Col. 1:15). However, he is also the one in whom "all the fullness of God was pleased to dwell" (Col. 1:19). Jesus is the perfect Adamic image and representative of God because he is God himself. This is not to say that Mark narrates the transfiguration to make this precise theological point, but we are again reminded that the rigid distinction between Jesus as human and Jesus as divine is not as neat as some make out.

The second aspect of the event to consider is the presence of Moses and Elijah. Many think that Moses and Elijah represent the Law and the Prophets. Yet, this is unlikely: (1) note that the initial order "Elijah with Moses" (Mark 9:4) has the two reversed; (2) Elijah was not a writing prophet; (3) when Elijah's role is discussed in 9:11–13, it is not his role as a prophet.[35] More likely is that both were key to Jewish end-time hopes. Malachi 4:5 anticipated Elijah's return before the end. Similarly, in Deuteronomy 18:15–19 Moses promised that a prophet like him would come. Furthermore, both Moses and Elijah had significant mountain-top encounters with God.[36] The presence of Moses and Elijah then point to Jesus's reign as the "messianic Son who brings to fulfilment the promises of God."[37]

33 Schnabel, *Mark*, 209.
34 Stein, *Mark*, 417.
35 France, *Gospel of Mark*, 351.
36 Schnabel, *Mark*, 210.
37 Schnabel, *Mark*, 210.

The final aspect of the passage that contributes to our picture of Jesus is the voice from heaven. Following Peter's suggestion to build three shelters, the voice from the cloud (symbolizing God's presence as the pillar of cloud did in the exodus) responds, "This is my beloved Son; listen to him" (Mark 9:7). The description of Jesus as God's beloved Son echoes his baptism (1:11). These words at the very least pick up the promises of a Davidic king in the Old Testament (cf. 2 Sam. 7:14; Ps. 2:7). The description of Jesus as the *beloved* Son alludes to Abraham's (aborted) sacrifice of Isaac (Gen. 22:2). The command to "listen to him" recalls Moses's instruction to the people of Israel to listen to the prophet who would come (Deut. 18:15).

As noted above, the transfiguration follows Jesus telling the disciples that some of them would see the kingdom after it had "come with power" (Mark 9:1). What they see is Jesus in his glory, flanked by Moses and Elijah and affirmed by God as his beloved Son. This underlines two aspects of the kingdom for us.

First, the focus of the kingdom is the Lord Jesus. The disciples were not, as John later was, granted a vision of "a new heaven and a new earth" (Rev. 21:1) but a vision of the glorified Jesus. As we saw with the beginning of Mark, Jesus brings the kingdom, and so this glimpse of the kingdom appropriately centers on him.

Second, the kingdom coming with power is revealed by the *glorified* Lord Jesus. The transfiguration, then, shows that the kingdom of God is a new-creation reality. The disciples see Jesus in his future, risen, new-creation glory, for Christ through his resurrection will bring in the kingdom. Mark's account of the resurrection is sparse compared to the other Gospels, but with his account of the transfiguration he points to the future reality of God's kingdom with the risen, glorified Christ at the center. What Mark narrates here strongly resonates with Paul's portrait of the future (e.g., Rom. 8:29; 1 Cor. 15:23–24, 40–44). The connection is particularly strong with 1 Corinthians where Paul presents the risen Christ as a new Adam (1 Cor. 15:45). Here we find the new Adam, the glorified Lord Jesus, the head of a new humanity.

Conclusion

What is the kingdom of God? Typically, it is defined in generic, abstract terms like "the reign of God." However, for Mark the kingdom is tangible.[38] Mark's Gospel ties the kingdom to two concrete realities—Jesus Christ and the new creation. Mark does not offer a definition. By combining these two emphases, however, he shows that God's kingdom is the new creation with Jesus Christ at its center.

The arrival of Jesus at the beginning of the Gospel means that the kingdom has drawn near. The tension between present and future aspects of the kingdom lies in the fact that the new creation has not fully begun—for Jesus in his earthly ministry or the world. However, in his miracles—particularly his healings and his exorcisms—Jesus offers a foretaste of the new creation in which there will be neither evil nor sickness. As we move through Mark's Gospel, we see the emphasis on the presence of the kingdom (e.g., 1:15) give way to an emphasis on its future coming (e.g., 13:34, 14:25). This corresponds to the presence of Jesus himself—as Mark's Gospel unfolds, his departure becomes more prominent.

For Mark, the *fullest* expression of the kingdom of God is seen in the new creation. It is not simply that the kingdom of God *is* the new creation. It exists even now (a point Jesus makes in his parables), but its fullest expression lies in the future. This idea of the kingdom as the new creation with Jesus Christ at the center animates Jesus's statement in 14:25: "I will not drink again of the fruit of the vine until that day when I drink it new in the kingdom of God." The picture is of Jesus celebrating with his people in the new creation.

Understanding the kingdom this way helps explain the relative lack of reference to the kingdom in other New Testament writings. While "kingdom" language may be less common outside of the Synoptic

---

38 I am indebted to my friend, former teacher, and former colleague, Peter Bolt, for first helping me to see that the kingdom is not a vague and abstract idea but a concrete, life-and-death reality.

Gospels, references to the risen Lord Jesus and the new creation abound. For example, Paul brings the ideas of kingdom, Christ, and new creation together in Colossians. The kingdom of God is "the kingdom of his beloved Son" (Col. 1:13). He is the "firstborn of all creation" (Col. 1:15) and "the firstborn from the dead" (Col. 1:18).

Repent and Believe the Gospel

Salvation through Jesus

ONE OF THE CHALLENGES of exploring different themes in Mark is that each interlocks with the others. Nowhere is this more evident than with the topics of salvation, discipleship, and Jesus's death. This chapter will concentrate on the theme of salvation from the point of view of the believer and will answer the question, what is the believer's role in salvation? The overlap with discipleship steps forward at this point, since the answer to this question seems straightforward: follow Jesus. The center of Mark's Gospel is Jesus's call to follow him to death: "Whoever loses his life for my sake and the gospel's will save it" (Mark 8:35).

However, this call to follow Jesus points to a tension at the heart of Mark. By the end of the Gospel, every one the twelve has failed to follow Jesus to the cross—all have abandoned him. How, then, is salvation possible if even the closest followers fail to meet his sole condition?[1] Furthermore, does salvation by discipleship not clash with the Pauline concept of justification by faith alone (e.g., Rom. 3:28; 4:5)? To answer these questions, I will examine Mark's Gospel in a way that reveals its deeper structure of salvation, one that offers hope even to

---

1 This is the question posed by Gabi Markusse, *Salvation in the Gospel of Mark: The Death of Jesus and the Path of Discipleship* (Eugene, OR: Pickwick, 2018).

failed disciples. Discipleship and salvation are inextricably linked but
are not identical.

The Expectation of Salvation

The theme of salvation is introduced at the start. Mark presents his work,
as we have seen, as "the beginning of the gospel" (Mark 1:1), which for
early Christians would have been associated with salvation (Paul says
the gospel is "the power of God for salvation," Rom. 1:16, and describes
it as "the gospel of your salvation," Eph. 1:13). Then in the following two
verses Mark quotes from the Old Testament. Although the cited words
do not mention salvation, examining the quotation in its Old Testament
context(s) shows that Mark situates his work within a salvific framework.

Mark introduces the citation as "written in Isaiah the prophet."
However, no passage in Isaiah has this form of words. In fact, as most
scholars agree, this quotation combines material from Malachi 3:1,
Isaiah 40:3, and possibly Exodus 23:20. We can't be certain why Mark
identifies the source as simply "Isaiah";[2] however, this would not have
worried the original readers.[3] In any case, although Mark has included
elements from other passages, he wants us to read the citation in the
light of the prophet Isaiah. He does so to indicate "that the conceptual
framework for his Gospel is the Isaianic new exodus."[4]

Isaiah 40:3, which makes up a major part of the quotation, comes
at a crossroads in the book of Isaiah, where the prophecy shifts from
indictment to hope. Isaiah 40 opens with a call by God to "comfort,
comfort my people" (Isa. 40:1). Throughout the next fifteen chapters,
Israel's *future* deliverance from Babylon is predicted using the language
and patterns of the *past* exodus. For example, as the people "go out"
(Isa. 52:11), the Lord promises to go "before" them and be their "rear

---

2   For a brief survey, see Rikk E. Watts, "Mark," in *Commentary on the New Testament Use of the Old Testament*, ed. G. K. Beale and D. A. Carson (Grand Rapids, MI: Baker Academic, 2007), 114.

.   3   For example, there is some evidence of a common Jewish practice of identifying a composite collection of texts by one author (see Watts, "Mark," 114).

4   Richard B. Hays, *Echoes of Scripture in the Gospels* (Waco, TX: Baylor University Press, 2016), 21.

guard" (Isa. 52:12). They will "pass through the waters" (Isa. 43:2), for the Lord "makes a way in the sea" (Isa. 43:16). He will cause "chariot and horse, army and warrior" to "lie down" so that "they cannot rise" (Isa. 43:17). He "will make a way in the wilderness" and "give water in the wilderness . . . to my chosen people" (Isa. 43:19–20).[5] Within these chapters, Isaiah 40:3 establishes the agenda, for "without Yahweh's presence (cf. Isa. 40:5, 9, 10, 11) there can be no salvation. It is his advent as a mighty warrior that is the sine qua non of Israel's deliverance."[6] However, despite their similarities, this new exodus will so far surpass the original one that the former event will be forgotten (Isa. 40:18–19).

While the Lord, to be sure, brought his exiles back from Babylon, this second exodus fell short of the grand promises made in Isaiah. Hence, later prophets like Malachi look ahead to when these promises will be fully realized. A main feature of these promises is the Lord's presence among his people. The promise of Malachi 3:1 ("Behold, I send my messenger, and he will prepare the way before me") thus naturally connects to Isaiah 40–55 in announcing a forerunner before the coming of the Lord. Mark understands that the coming of John the Baptist fulfills this anticipation. Malachi and Isaiah both anticipate that the one following the messenger will be God himself ("my" and "me" in Mal. 3:1; "the LORD" and "our God" in Isa. 40:3). Mark sees this promised coming of God fulfilled in the person of Jesus. "Christologically speaking, the striking identification of Jesus (Mark 1:1) with Yahweh's coming (1:2–3) can hardly be missed."[7]

Mark's first scriptural quotation orients us to his Gospel in three ways. First, it directs us to Jesus's identity. He comes to fulfill the promise of divine presence not as a substitute for God but as God himself. Second, it speaks of his mission. He comes to fulfill the long-promised second exodus. The narrative proper opens "in the wilderness" with John preaching a "baptism of repentance for the forgiveness of sins" (1:4). All of Judea and Jerusalem "were going out" to John (1:5). This

---

5   These examples are drawn from Watts, "Mark," 114.

6   Watts, "Mark," 114.

7   Watts, "Mark," 120.

exodus, or "going out,"[8] differs from the original one. Rather than the people going out from Egypt, traveling through the wilderness, and entering Israel, they now leave Israel, travel to the wilderness to be baptized, and then return to Israel.[9] Third, combining these two aspects, the quotation reminds us that salvation is a divine work. The Lord himself has arrived to save his people—to bring forgiveness (Isa. 40:2; cf. Mark 1:4; 2:10). Keeping this initial orientation in mind is important as we see the disciples fail. Rather than questioning the possibility of salvation, their failure stresses their inability and thus the need for God to save. Jesus will teach concerning salvation, "With man it is impossible, but not with God. For all things are possible with God" (Mark 10:27).

Salvation and Baptism

Mark's narrative begins with John baptizing. The messenger promised in Isaiah 40:3 comes preaching a message about Jesus (Mark 1:7–8), but before he does that, he speaks of *baptism*—a baptism "of repentance for the forgiveness of sins" (1:4). This message concerning baptism continues to orient us as readers to Mark's framework of salvation.

John's expression "baptism of repentance" (*baptisma metanoias*) is a genitive construction in which the second noun describes the first—that is, a "repentance baptism." In other words, John calls for a repentance marked by baptism.[10] In this way, baptism expresses the repentance that has taken place.

Baptism's link to repentance informs the next verse: "All the country of Judea and all Jerusalem were going out to him and were being baptized by him in the river Jordan, confessing their sins" (1:5). John's baptism became the occasion for expressing their repentance by confessing their sins. John's preaching was infused with two elements:

---

8   The same Greek verb (*ekporeuomai*) is used in the LXX to refer to the exodus. See, e.g., Ex. 13:4.

9   This insight is not mine, but I cannot find its source. I suspect that I heard it in a sermon or a podcast.

10 So Mark L. Strauss, *Mark*, ZECNT (Grand Rapids, MI: Zondervan Academic, 2014), 64; Robert H. Stein, *Mark*, BECNT (Grand Rapids, MI: Baker Academic, 2008), 45.

repentance (1:4–5) and the coming of Christ (1:7–8), which suggests that repentance is necessary "not because this is what God has always demanded but because of the christological and eschatological events that are taking place."[11]

John the Baptist (1:4) and Jesus (1:15) both speak about repentance— a turning around. Repentance is neither developed nor frequently referred to in Mark; however, the later stress on discipleship flows from this initial turning. The kingdom brings in such radically new values (e.g., 10:31) that a lifetime of repentance is appropriate.[12] Jesus teaches that the parables serve as a means of judgment so that those on the outside would remain on the outside and

> may indeed see but not perceive,
>   and may indeed hear but not understand,
> lest they should turn [*epistrepsōsin*] and be forgiven. (4:12)

Even though the main stress in this saying is on the sovereign hardening of God, the implication remains: forgiveness follows turning.

In 1:7 John's message focuses on Jesus as the mightier one who comes after him. If Jesus surpasses John, then it is no surprise that Jesus's baptism is also greater: while John baptized with water, the coming one will baptize "with the Holy Spirit" (1:8). How should we understand Jesus's baptizing "with" or "in"[13] the Holy Spirit? His baptism brings the reality that John's baptism only anticipated: the Spirit, the presence of the age to come. The context of the Old Testament quotation in 1:2–3 points to Jesus's divine identity. This is confirmed in his ability to baptize with the Holy Spirit. Isaiah 44:3 relates Yahweh as promising, "I will pour my Spirit upon your offspring."

11 Stein, *Mark*, 45.
12 R. T. France, *The Gospel of Mark: A Commentary on the Greek Text*, NIGTC (Grand Rapids, MI: Eerdmans, 2002), 66–67.
13 The Greek preposition *en* is probably too broad to make too precise a distinction here. So France, *Mark*, 72.

Mark's account of Jesus's baptism is shorter than Matthew's (Matt. 3:13–17), and we don't learn why Jesus submitted to John's baptism (i.e., "to fulfill all righteousness" in Matt. 3:15). We are left to infer from the flow of the narrative that submission to John's baptism indicates that Jesus "identified with John's message of Israel's need of repentance for the forgiveness of sins and the expectation of imminent restoration through the outpouring of God's Spirit."[14]

At Jesus's baptism, three things happen: the heavens are "torn open" (Mark 1:10); the Spirit descends on him "like a dove" (1:10); and a voice from heaven states, "You are my beloved Son; with you I am well pleased" (1:11). The tearing open of the heavens perhaps anticipates the tearing of the curtain in the temple (15:38) and serves as a fulfillment of Isaiah 64:1 where the prophet prays, "Oh that you would rend the heavens and come down."[15] There, as here, God's in-breaking presence is associated with the presence of the Holy Spirit (Isa. 63:10, 14). The Spirit's descent is, again, narrated with less commentary than in other Gospels (cf. the observation in John 1:32 that the Spirit *remained* on Jesus). Here the emphasis falls on the simple fact of his being anointed with the Spirit. The one who will baptize with the Spirit receives an anointing with the Spirit at his own baptism.

Jesus undergoes another baptism in Mark's Gospel. In Mark 10, James and John ask Jesus for the honor of sitting "one at your right hand and one at your left, in your glory" (10:37). He tells them they are ignorant of what they ask and then adds, "Are you able to drink the cup that I drink, or to be baptized with the baptism with which I am baptized?" (10:38). They respond that they are able. Jesus tells them that while he cannot decide who will sit at his right or his left, they will indeed drink the same cup and be baptized with the baptism that he himself will undergo. In using the imagery of the "cup" and his

---

14   Eckhard J. Schnabel, *Mark: An Introduction and Commentary*, TNTC (Downers Grove, IL: IVP Academic, 2017), 45.

15   Although the verb is different in the LXX of Isa. 64:1, Hays (*Echoes of Scripture in the Gospels*, 18) suggests that Mark's "more vivid verb offers a stronger allusion" to the underlying Hebrew of Isaiah.

"baptism," Jesus refers again to his death, which he has addressed in 10:33–34.[16] If Mark here associates baptism with Jesus's death, it seems reasonable to see the earlier account of his baptism as anticipating that subsequent event.

The voice of God from heaven similarly connects Jesus's baptism with his death. God tells Jesus, "You are my beloved Son; with you I am well pleased" (1:11). This language echoes Genesis 22 where God tells Abraham to sacrifice his beloved son (LXX Gen. 22:2: *ton huion sou ton agapēton*; cf. 22:12, 16).[17] The similar description of Jesus in Mark 1:11 (*ho huios mou ho agapētos*) suggests an allusion to Jesus's sacrificial death. The reader is invited "to understand God as the father who will not spare his own son even as Abraham did not spare Isaac" (Gen. 22:12).[18] The one being baptized is the Spirit-anointed Son of God who will die for his people. The baptism introduces "the two-pronged messianic identity that it will take the duration of the story to fully disclose: Jesus is the Christ, but his particular calling as Christ means to be rejected, suffer, die, and rise again."[19]

Baptism in Mark, then, speaks of Jesus's death and the gift of the Spirit. In Jesus's first baptism (by John) he receives the Spirit. This anticipates his second baptism (his death) when he gives the Spirit (i.e., baptizes with the Spirit). Mark's theology here corresponds to Paul's in Galatians 3. Christ died "so that we might receive the promised Spirit through faith" (Gal. 3:14). Christ's death secures the gift of the Spirit. Furthermore, Paul associates salvation with baptism into Christ and putting on Christ (Gal. 3:27). In Romans he expands on this notion of being baptized into Christ (Rom. 6:3). In 1 Corinthians he associates it with receiving the Spirit (1 Cor. 12:13).

Mark is presenting the story of salvation. In Mark 1:2–3, he generates the expectation that this salvation would be a divine initiative.

16 France, *Mark*, 416; Schnabel, *Mark*, 251.
17 J. R. Daniel Kirk, *A Man Attested by God: The Human Jesus of the Synoptic Gospels* (Grand Rapids, MI: Eerdmans, 2016), 189.
18 Kirk, *A Man Attested*, 189.
19 Kirk, *A Man Attested*, 190.

Jesus's baptism highlights the role his death and the Spirit play in this salvation.

Salvation and Forgiveness

In announcing forgiveness of sins, John the Baptist appears as the messenger of Isaiah 40:3. This coming messenger in Isaiah is described in the context of the forgiveness of sins being announced for Israel—"that her iniquity is pardoned, that she has received from the LORD's hand double for all her sins" (Isa. 40:2). Already Isaiah had announced that the presence of the Lord "our king" leads to the people being "forgiven their iniquity" (33:22–24). For Isaiah, God's saving presence means the presence of forgiveness.

The structure of Mark highlights forgiveness. Peter Bolt has helpfully shown how the first main section (1:16–4:34) divides into four subsections each marked by Jesus's location next to the sea (1:16; 2:13; 3:7; 4:1).[20] Each subsection contains a call of some sort: Simon and his brothers in 1:16–20, Levi in 2:16, the twelve in 3:13, and "he who has ears to hear" in 4:9. Bolt suggests that forgiveness of sins is central to each subsection.

The first subsection (1:16–2:12) climaxes with Jesus confronting the scribes concerning his authority as the Son of Man to forgive sins (2:1–10). Although nothing suggests that the paralyzed man's condition resulted from his sin, the account underlines a relationship between sin and sickness that already appears in the Old Testament. Deuteronomy warned that if Israel failed to keep the law, God would bring on them "extraordinary afflictions, afflictions severe and lasting, and sicknesses grievous and lasting" (Deut. 28:59). The prophets extended the metaphor by speaking of Israel as a nation afflicted with sickness. Israel's "whole head is sick" and "whole heart faint"; from "the sole of the foot even to the head, there is no soundness" (Isa. 1:5–6). In fact, "her wound is incurable" (Mic. 1:9). Jeremiah says of the nation,

---

20 Peter Bolt, "'With a View to the Forgiveness of Sins': Jesus and Forgiveness in Mark's Gospel," *RTR* 57, no. 2 (1998): 58.

There is none to uphold your cause,
> no medicine for your wound,
> no healing for you. (Jer. 30:13)

It is only the Lord who can bring healing (Jer. 33:6; cf. Ex. 15:26).

Thus, Jesus's healings point to the sinfulness of the people and his identity as the divine healer—that is, the one who can bring forgiveness. Mark's healing accounts point to Israel's spiritual state and Jesus's ability to deal with the root cause of sickness—namely, sin. As Bolt concludes, "If sickness was a metaphor for Israel's sin and judgment, the metaphor for the reversal of this sorry state was obvious."[21]

The second subsection (2:13–3:6) "shows Jesus modelling the forgiveness he has brought to the land by eating with sinners."[22] It presents Jesus connecting sin and sickness: the one who has come to call sinners compares himself to a physician whom the sick need (2:17). In the third subsection (3:7–3:35), Jesus promises that "all sins will be forgiven" but warns, "Whoever blasphemes against the Holy Spirit never has forgiveness" (3:28–29). Finally, in the fourth subsection (4:1–34), Jesus teaches in parables and explains the purpose: that those outside would *not* perceive and understand "lest they should turn and be forgiven" (4:12).

Although the language of forgiveness occurs less frequently in the rest of the Gospel, Jesus continues to heal and exorcise demons, showing his ability to deal with Israel's sin. The sole mention of forgiveness after Mark 4 appears in 11:25 and concerns one's forgiveness of others. The rationale for forgiving anyone who has wronged you is "so that your Father also who is in heaven may forgive you your trespasses." Forgiving each other is connected to God's forgiveness.

Alongside forgiveness, we find a broader conception of salvation in the first section of Mark. Several times when Jesus heals someone, the verb used for "heal" is not *therapeuō* but *sōzō*—the verb typically used in the rest of the New Testament for "save," particularly in Paul

---

21 Bolt, "With a View to the Forgiveness of Sins," 63.
22 Bolt, "With a View to the Forgiveness of Sins," 65.

(e.g., Rom. 5:9; 1 Cor. 1:18). *Sōzō* denotes salvation or rescue—from death, illness, or eternal destruction. However, with this word, Mark maintains the symbolic connection between physical illness and sin, and Jesus's ability to solve the problem of sin.

In the first half of Mark, *sōzō* appears exclusively in the context of healing (Mark 3:4; 5:23, 28, 34; 6:56). Mark uses the more focused word for healing (*therapeuō*) only once, when members of the synagogue watch Jesus "to see whether he would heal" a man with a withered hand "on the Sabbath, so that they might accuse him" (3:2). Jesus challenges them, "Is it lawful on the Sabbath to do good or to do harm, to save [*sōsai*] life or to kill?" (3:4). How does healing a man with a crippled hand save a life? Jesus's parallelism suggests a broader issue than simply healing this man on the Sabbath. To "the degree that he brings wholeness to this crippled man by restoring his hand and his relationship with God, he brings to reality God's promised intent at creation."[23] That is, doing "good and saving life" overturns "the curse of the fall and the disease and sickness that resulted from the fall."[24]

The interwoven accounts of the woman subjected to bleeding and Jairus's daughter (5:21–43) further develop this connection between salvation and healing. As his daughter lies near death, Jairus implores Jesus to put his hands on her so that she might be "made well [*sōthē*] and live" (5:23). As Collins points out, while "Jairus seeks his daughter's rescue from death," as readers "who know the Gospel as a whole" we can "infer a second level of meaning relating to eternal life in the kingdom of God."[25]

The woman with the discharge of blood knows, "If I touch even his garments, I will be made well [*sōthēsomai*]" (5:28). When she does so, Jesus tells her, "Your faith has made you well [*sesōken*]" (5:34). The woman's faith reflects her deep conviction that Jesus can heal her.[26]

---

23 Robert A. Guelich, *Mark 1–8:26*, WBC (Dallas: Word, 1989), 136.
24 Stein, *Mark*, 155.
25 Adela Yarbro Collins, *Mark: A Commentary on the Gospel of Mark*, Hermeneia (Minneapolis: Fortress, 2007), 279. There may be a parallel between Jesus's description of the girl as "not dead but sleeping" (Mark 5:39) and Paul's description of the "dead in Christ" as "those who have fallen asleep" (1 Thess. 4:15–16).
26 France, *Mark*, 238.

Of course, *sōzō* refers here to physical healing, but as we have seen in the wider context of Mark and the Bible as a whole, physical healing connects to and symbolizes spiritual healing. The two senses of *sōzō* "certainly shade together, since faith is the prerequisite for both spiritual and physical restoration."[27] Asking whether a particular instance of *sōzō* refers to physical or spiritual healing somewhat misses the point, for as we see in the section above, physical sickness symbolizes spiritual sickness.

After Peter's confession at the midpoint of Mark, we discover a more obviously spiritual or eternal sense of *sōzō* when Jesus, speaking of the salvation of the soul, says, "Whoever loses his life for my sake and the gospel's will save [*sōsai*] it" (8:35). He then adds that nothing one gains, not even the whole world, compares to one's soul (8:36) and that nothing can be given to secure one's soul (8:37). The end of Mark 8 indicates that Jesus thinks not merely in physical terms, as though a person's life is the most valuable thing he has. No, this is a matter of end-time judgment. To lose one's soul equates with the Son of Man being ashamed of that person "when he comes in the glory of his Father with the holy angels" (8:38). Jesus thus connects (via the idea of a person's soul) salvation (*sōzō*) and end-time judgment much like Paul in, for example, Romans 5:9. The corollary, then, is that to save one's soul a person must be unashamed of Jesus and must lose his life for the sake of Jesus and the gospel (Mark 8:35).

The next use of *sōzō* appears in the account of Jesus and the rich man who asks what he must do to inherit eternal life (10:17–31). His question concerns final salvation. Jesus tells him (implicitly at least) to keep the commandments. When the man says he has done so, Jesus tells him that he lacks one thing: "sell all that you have and give to the poor, and you will have treasure in heaven; and come, follow me" (10:21).

This man, who "had great possessions," refuses Jesus who then turns to his disciples and tells them, "How difficult it will be for those who have wealth to enter the kingdom of God!" (10:22–23). Entering the kingdom is not just difficult for the rich, though, as Jesus widens

27 Strauss, *Mark*, 232.

the scope and says, "How difficult it is to enter the kingdom of God!" (10:24). However, he then returns to the question of the wealthy: "It is easier for a camel to go through the eye of a needle than for a rich person to enter the kingdom of God" (10:25). The disciples are astonished and ask, "Then who can be saved [sōthēnai]?" (10:26). "If this man—who has apparently kept the commandments his whole life and who has been blessed by God with great riches—cannot be saved, then who can?"[28] Jesus replies, "With man it is impossible, but not with God. For all things are possible with God" (10:27).

What exactly makes it impossible for humans to be saved? Does Jesus speak of our inability to "merit salvation" or "to respond to God's invitation"?[29] On balance, it seems that Mark is "simply content to emphasize to his readers that salvation involves God's gracious activity without being specific."[30]

After this account we have another use of sōzō to denote physical healing when Jesus restores the sight of Bartimaeus, a blind man. Twice we read that he cries out to Jesus with the words, "Son of David, have mercy on me" (10:47, 48). Before healing him, Jesus tells him, "Go your way; your faith has made you well [sesōken]" (10:52)—that is, Jesus "saves" him but does not call him to follow. Bartimaeus follows anyway, but the interaction shows that there is no simple correspondence between salvation and the kind of following to which Jesus calls the twelve. Not everyone Jesus saves is called to follow in the same way.

In the apocalyptic discourse of Mark 13, Jesus warns the disciples that they "will be hated by all" because of him, but he encourages them that "the one who endures to the end will be saved [sōthēsetai]" (13:13). This refers to eschatological salvation rather than physical healing/deliverance. The end essentially refers to the end of the disciples' lives. Salvation depends on perseverance.[31]

---

28 Strauss, *Mark*, 444.
29 Stein, *Mark*, 473.
30 Stein, *Mark*, 473.
31 Strauss (*Mark*, 577) notes parallels in Rom. 8:17; 1 Cor. 9:25; 2 Tim. 4:8; Heb. 10:36; James 1:12; 1 Pet. 5:4; Rev. 2:7, 10, 17, 26–28; 3:5, 12, 21; 20:4.

In the same speech Jesus warns of the tribulation to come and, speaking proleptically, says, "If the Lord had not cut short the days, no human being would be saved [*esōthē*]. But for the sake of the elect, whom he chose, he shortened the days" (13:20). Reference to the "elect," *eklektos*, occurs only in this section of Mark (see also 13:22, 27) and links with Paul's teaching that the elect will be saved (see, e.g., Rom. 8:33; 2 Tim. 2:10; Titus 1:1). The Old Testament uses similar terminology when God speaks of his people whom he has "chosen" using the cognate verb *eklegomai* (e.g., Ps. 33:12; Isa. 41:8). Some, therefore, find in these words a reference to the destruction of Jerusalem and the salvation of Jewish Christians in particular. However, the broader language of Mark 13:27—"and then he will send out the angels and gather his elect from the four winds, from the ends of the earth to the ends of heaven"—suggests that "elect" refers to Christians—both Jew and Gentile.

The final use of *sōzō* occurs at the cross. The passersby deride Jesus and challenge him, "Save [*sōson*] yourself, and come down from the cross!" (15:30). The chief priests and the scribes add to the torment by pointing out, "He saved [*esōsen*] others; he cannot save [*sōsai*] himself" (15:31). Again, Mark ties salvation to Jesus's death. He emphasizes the connection by presenting two groups that challenge Jesus to extricate himself from the cross. But, "for Jesus to save himself would be the very thing that would keep him from saving (in the ultimate sense) others, for he must pour out his life in sacrifice as a ransom for many (10:45; 14:24)."[32] The "irony of the Markan drama is that by staying on the cross, Jesus is fulfilling the role of the Messiah, bringing salvation to Israel by offering his life as a ransom for sins (10:45)."[33]

Salvation and Faith

So far I have concentrated on the divine aspect of salvation—the coming of the Lord who will die, give the Spirit, and bring forgiveness and salvation for the people. We saw in chapter 2 that revelation must be

---

32 Stein, *Mark*, 714.
33 Strauss, *Mark*, 694.

received. It must be met by genuine sight, genuine hearing, and an understanding heart. Salvation is the same—it is to be received by faith. Jesus initially said that people should "repent and believe in the gospel" (1:15). Then, when he saw the faith of the paralytic's friends, for example, he pronounced sins forgiven (2:5).

Frequently people are healed/saved (*sōzō*) because they believe, such as the woman with the discharge of blood (5:34) and blind Bartimaeus (10:52). In 4:40 he rebukes the disciples for their fear of the storm and asks, "Have you still no faith?" Here the enemy of faith is not ignorance but fear. Similarly, he encourages Jairus to "not fear, only believe" (5:36). Although this command to believe does not have a named object, in Mark's Gospel faith is directed toward a message (the gospel in 1:15; a false message about Christ in 13:21), a messenger (John the Baptist in 11:31), Jesus (2:5), and God (11:24).[34] In 5:36 Jesus directs Jairus to believe in him.

In 6:6 in his hometown, Jesus is amazed at people's lack of faith. He also gently rebukes the father of the demon-possessed boy who questions Jesus's ability to heal his son (9:22). Jesus tells him, "All things are possible for one who believes," prompting the boy's father to cry out, "I believe; help my unbelief!" (9:23–24). Collins assumes too much when she interprets Jesus's statement to mean that faith "is a quality that can endow human beings with divine power."[35] For it is *not* the father who exercises or is endowed with divine power. He believes, but *Jesus* heals the boy. This has led to the perhaps clumsy suggestion that Jesus's words should be translated: "All things [are] able [to be done] for the one who believes."[36]

Jesus revisits the notion that anything is possible for those who believe when he tells the disciples, "Have faith in God" (11:22). Even if one told a mountain to be thrown into the sea, if that person "does not doubt in his heart, but believes that what he says will come to pass,

34 Stein, *Mark*, 272.

35 Collins, *Mark*, 438.

36 R. H. Gundry, *Mark: A Commentary on His Apology for the Cross* (Grand Rapids, MI: Eerdmans, 1992), 499, cited in Stein, *Mark*, 434.

it will be done for him" (11:23). Although Jesus refers to a particular mountain here (probably the Temple Mount given the destruction of the temple in Mark 13—although perhaps the Mount of Olives is in view), the point is that mountain moving points to "something humanly impossible, but possible with God (cf. Zech. 4:7)."[37] This leads to the promise that "whatever you ask in prayer, believe that you have received it, and it will be yours" (Mark 11:24).

Jesus describes children as "little ones who believe in me" and warns of the dangers of leading them into sin (9:42). Although in context Jesus seems to refer to literal children (cf. 9:36–37), the "little ones" probably include Jesus's followers more generally. Certainly, any Christian is susceptible to sin, but we note the almost incidental description: "little ones who *believe* in me." Belief in Jesus is the essence of what it means to be a Christian.

The final reference to faith comes in 15:32 when the chief priests and scribes mock Jesus, challenging him to come from the cross "that we may see and believe." By including their words, Mark implicitly critiques them and places faith in opposition to unbelieving, purely physical sight (cf. 2 Cor. 5:7).

Suzanne Watts Henderson compares faith in Mark and John. John writes so that his readers might "believe that Jesus is the Christ, the Son of God" (John 20:31). In contrast, "the dividing line in Mark's gospel concerns not the precise affirmation of Jesus's identity (belief that Jesus is the Christ) but, rather, a resolute affirmation that, through Jesus, God's dominion is taking hold of the world (trust in the messianic mission he embodies)."[38] This is helpful, although Henderson goes too far when she asserts that "faith is never explicitly described as faith 'in Jesus.'"[39] While the phrase "faith in Jesus" or its equivalent never appears, faith is repeatedly directed to him. Furthermore, as noted, a Christian can be described as a "little one who believes in me" (Mark 9:42).

37 Strauss, *Mark*, 499.
38 Suzanne Watts Henderson, *Christology and Discipleship in the Gospel of Mark*, SNTSMS 135 (Cambridge, UK: Cambridge University Press, 2006), 12.
39 Henderson, *Christology and Discipleship*, 12n31.

For Mark, faith unlocks the door "for participation in the dawning kingdom (1:14f) and for appropriation of its unlimited powers (9:23)."[40] This "attitude of perceptive dependence" alone is "capable of receiving Jesus's deeds as revelatory acts of God."[41] Faith never reduces to cognition, but it cannot be separated from it. It is "grounded upon an intuitive or revelatory insight into the identity of Jesus as bearer of God's eschatological power and mercy."[42] Although the nature of salvation and even the "content" of the faith are less explicitly developed than in the rest of the New Testament, nevertheless saving faith is directed to Jesus.

Conclusion

This chapter began by highlighting the profound tension that Mark raises in connection with salvation. Jesus summons his disciples to follow him to the cross, telling them that if they want to save their lives, they need to lose them. None of them, however, are willing to. Indeed, by the end of Mark, Jesus goes to the cross alone, for all have abandoned him.

However, the disciples' failure underlines the truth concerning salvation: what is impossible for human beings is possible for God (Mark 10:27). Salvation is ultimately a divine act. Mark introduces this theme by citing Isaiah 40:3. Jesus's coming into the world fulfills the promise that Yahweh would come to bring the promised new exodus—the final exodus that ultimately ushers in the new creation. Jesus comes as Yahweh, but he also comes as a human. He submits to John's baptism and receives the Spirit, pointing forward to his submission to the baptism of death and his subsequent giving of the Spirit—fulfilling the promise of Isaiah 44:3.

Chapter 7 will explore the death of Jesus in order to sharpen our understanding of its saving impact. At this stage, we can draw a parallel

---

40 Christopher D. Marshall, *Faith as a Theme in Mark's Narrative*, SNTSMS 64 (Cambridge, UK: Cambridge University Press, 1989), 234.

41 Marshall, *Faith as a Theme*, 234.

42 Marshall, *Faith as a Theme*, 235.

with the observations from chapter 3 when we looked at revelation. Revelation must be seen and perceived, which is only possible through Jesus's intervention. Salvation, likewise, must be received—by faith. Faith unlocks God's power (Mark 11:23), bringing forgiveness (2:5) and salvation (5:34).

The role of the Spirit is not developed, although we have seen that he is presented as foundational for salvation. Jesus will baptize with the Spirit, even though this event is not narrated in the Gospel. Again if we read Mark as outlining the "beginning of the gospel," we understand that the Spirit fulfills the role that Jesus performs in Mark—opening people's eyes so that they can respond in faith.

For Paul, the gospel is "the power of God for salvation to everyone who believes" (Rom. 1:16). Mark, like Paul, presents salvation by faith in terms of forgiveness in this life and eternal life in the age to come. Mark does not use the language of justification (cf. Luke 18:14), but like Paul he highlights forgiveness (Mark 2:10; cf. Rom. 4:5–7 and Paul's connection between justification and forgiveness).

As surely as Paul states it, so Mark narrates the connection between faith and salvation in the healing miracles. Israel is sick—afflicted by demons and disease—because of her sin. Jesus has come to heal and deliver those who believe. However, Mark's portrayal of salvation is not discrete. It is woven into faith, repentance, and baptism—both Jesus's own baptism and the baptism of those who turn to him (with the subsequent gift of the Holy Spirit). Mark's portrayal of salvation also connects to discipleship (the subject of the next chapter) and to the death and resurrection of Christ (the final chapter). Jesus saves people so that they might follow him. It won't do—as we have seen in this chapter—to say that salvation is *by* discipleship. But it is true—as we will see in the next chapter—to say that salvation is *for* discipleship.

A narrative of Jesus allows us to see what we cannot in an epistle: the dramatic effects of the salvation Jesus brings. A paralyzed man walks away after his encounter with Jesus; a man afflicted with so many demons that he was uncontrollable now sits in his right mind;

a woman who had bled for twelve years is restored after touching Jesus's garments; a dead girl is raised to life; the blind see and the deaf hear. The accounts enable us to *see* the "power of God for salvation" (Rom. 1:16). The kingdom of God has arrived in the person of Jesus, and with it comes the powerful salvation, healing, and restoration that he brings.

Follow Me

Being a Disciple of Jesus

THE LANGUAGE OF DISCIPLESHIP is unique to the Gospels and Acts. Outside of these first five books of the New Testament, the word for "disciple" (*mathētēs*) never appears. Although Mark's teaching concerning discipleship overlaps with various elements in the rest of the New Testament, its specific language shines a light on the uniqueness of Jesus's earthly ministry. While the way a believer in first-century Corinth (for example) followed Jesus was in continuity with how the twelve were called to follow him to the cross, we will see that there are significant differences. This should caution against a simplistic imitation of the experience of the first disciples.

In Mark 1, following Jesus's baptism, temptation, and initial proclamation of the gospel of God, he calls his disciples. He first summons Simon and his brother Andrew to follow him, promising to make them "fishers of men" (1:16–17). These two fishermen immediately leave their nets to follow Jesus. He then encounters James and his brother John and likewise calls them as they mend their nets. They too leave their fishing gear and follow Jesus (1:19–20). Mark 3 provides a more formal appointing of the twelve apostles[1] "so that they might be with

---

1   They are only identified as apostles in 3:14 and 6:30.

him and he might send them out to preach and have authority to cast out demons" (3:14–15). Finally, the twelve are commissioned to proclaim repentance and to cast out demons and heal the sick (6:7–13). This calling, appointing, commissioning, and sending establishes the nucleus of the new people of God. Mark also in this way introduces the theme of discipleship.

Jesus calls others in addition to the twelve. The language of "calling" (*kaleō* and cognate verbs *parakaleō* and *proskaleō*) is used of various people throughout the Gospel. Jesus calls the disciples (1:20; 3:13; 6:7), sinners rather than the righteous (2:17), people to listen to his teaching (3:23; 7:14; 10:42), and people to follow him (8:34). Although "calling does not bear heavy theological weight in Mark's Gospel . . . any meaningful interaction with Jesus involves both his initiative and people's response."[2]

Discipleship interacts with the other themes we have considered—particularly salvation and Christology. Regarding Christology, when Jesus calls his first disciples in Mark 1, their response is immediate, highlighting his authority. More specifically, the fact that Jesus calls them to leave their profession points to his divine identity since "it is only God who can command people to leave their profession with which they earn their livelihood in order to be devoted to his service."[3] This raises the question of continuity with the Old Testament. Does Jesus's model of discipleship resemble similar relationships in the Old Testament?

Discipleship in the Old Testament

On the surface, Jesus's calling of his disciples to be "fishers of men" (1:17) might appear to mimic the Old Testament. In Jeremiah 16:16, God says he is "sending for many fishers" to "catch" people (cf. Ezek. 29:4–5; 38:4; Amos 4:2; Hab. 1:14–17), but there the motif is one of judgment. God says he will send fishers followed by hunters to catch

---

2   Brenda B. Colijn, "Salvation as Discipleship in the Gospel of Mark," *ATJ* 30 (1998): 14.
3   Eckhard J. Schnabel, *Mark: An Introduction and Commentary*, TNTC (Downers Grove, IL: IVP Academic, 2017), 53.

his enemies since "they are not hidden from me, nor is their iniquity concealed from my eyes" (Jer. 16:17). Read in the light of Mark's Gospel (and even in the light of the immediate context of Mark 1:14–15), Jesus's imagery clearly denotes salvation: "To fish for people is to rescue them from sin and death by calling them into God's kingdom."[4] Jesus employs an everyday metaphor that these fishermen would have readily understood.[5]

The wider question remains: does Jesus's call to discipleship emerge from the Old Testament? The language of discipleship is largely absent from the Old Testament; the word *mathētēs* never appears in the LXX. Karl Rengstorf argues that not only is the word missing but the concept as well.[6] Apart "from the formal relation of teacher and pupil, the OT, unlike the classical Greek world and Hellenism, has no master-disciple relation."[7] He suggests that the concept of discipleship is foreign to the Old Testament because God alone is master and teacher. No human being, no matter how great, can function as a master for other human beings.[8]

However, although "disciple" language is absent from the Old Testament, the related concept of "following" is applied *both* to humans toward God *and* to humans toward their leaders. This is expressed in a variety of ways. Caleb "followed" (*epakaloutheō*) the Lord fully (LXX Num. 14:24).[9] Israel is said to "follow" (*aphēgeomai*) Moses (LXX Ex. 11:8). In the LXX, the preposition *opisō*—meaning "after" or "behind"—can express the relationship of following, whether following a person

---

4   Mark L. Strauss, *Mark*, ZECNT (Grand Rapids, MI: Zondervan Academic, 2014), 64; Robert H. Stein, *Mark*, BECNT (Grand Rapids, MI: Baker Academic, 2008), 83.

5   R. T. France, *The Gospel of Mark: A Commentary on the Greek Text*, NIGTC (Grand Rapids, MI: Eerdmans, 2002), 96.

6   Karl Heinrich Rengstorf, "Μανθάνω, Καταμανθάνω, Μαθητής, Συμμαθητής, Μαθήτρια, Μαθητεύω," in *Theological Dictionary of the New Testament*, ed. Gerhard Kittel, Geoffrey W. Bromiley, and Gerhard Friedrich, 10 vols. (Grand Rapids, MI: Eerdmans, 1964), 4:427–30.

7   Rengstorf, "Μανθάνω," 427.

8   Rengstorf, "Μανθάνω," 431.

9   Cf. LXX Num. 32:12 and Deut. 1:36, which speak similarly of Caleb but with different verbs for "follow."

(e.g., 2 Sam. 20:2, 11; 1 Kings 1:7) or following the Lord (e.g., 1 Kings 11:6; Isa. 59:13). When the people ask Samuel for a king, he tells them that it will be well "if both you and the king who reigns over you will follow ["go after," *opisō poreuomenoi*] the LORD your God" (1 Sam. 12:14). The Israelites who followed ("went after," *eporeuthē opisō*) the Baal of Peor were destroyed (Deut. 4:3). When Ishbosheth begins to reign over Israel, Judah followed ("were behind," *ēsan opisō*) David (2 Sam. 2:10). Later, people are described as following ("going after," *egenēthē opisō*) Absalom (2 Sam. 15:13). The clearest parallel to the disciples following Jesus is 1 Kings 19:20 where Elisha follows ("follow after," *akalouthēsō opisō*) Elijah.

So although the Greek word *mathētēs* is not found in the LXX, related terms nevertheless point to a disciple type of relationship. Furthermore, Michael Wilkins shows how the Hebrew word for "pupil" (*talmid*) can be used of relationships similar to that of discipleship in the New Testament. In 1 Chronicles 25:8 the musicians cast lots for their duties, "small and great, teacher and pupil alike." Whether or not this language of "pupil" indicates a formal school, at the very least it shows some musicians were "engaged in the learning process," perhaps as "an apprentice learning a trade."[10] Wilkins also considers the schools of prophets (e.g., 1 Sam. 10:5–10), the sons of prophets (e.g., 1 Kings 20:35), the scribes (e.g., 1 Chron. 2:55), and *possible* schools of wise men (e.g., Prov. 22:17). Isaiah 8 refers to Isaiah's disciples when he instructs, "Bind up the testimony; seal the teaching among my disciples" (Isa. 8:16).[11]

There are certainly antecedents to the discipleship relationship in Mark. The relationship that Jesus establishes nevertheless differs from disciple-master relationships in the Old Testament. In fact, the relationship to which he calls them more closely resembles the absolute call that God makes on Israel in the Old Testament.

---

10   Michael J. Wilkins, *Discipleship in the Ancient World and Matthew's Gospel*, 2nd ed. (Grand Rapids, MI: Baker, 1995), 46.
11   Although the Greek version is quite different as seen in the NETS translation: "Then shall become manifest those who seal up the law so that they might not learn."

Discipleship and the Disciples

Jesus first calls Simon and Andrew in Mark 1:17. This is noteworthy in that disciples usually approached a potential master.[12] He then calls James and John in 1:19; their immediate departure from their family underlines Jesus's authority over all of life—including family. While Elijah permits Elisha to bid farewell to his family, Jesus's disciples drop everything to follow him (cf. 1 Kings 19:19–21; Luke 9:57–62).

This theme of family reappears in Mark 3, where Jesus effectively redefines it in terms of relation to him, so that "whoever does the will of God, he is my brother and sister and mother" (3:35). Later he envisages people leaving "house or brothers or sisters or mother or father or children or lands, for [his] sake and for the gospel" (10:29). However, this redefinition of family is not absolute: he criticizes the Pharisees and scribes for allowing neglect of mother and father, thus overturning the word of God by their tradition (7:5–13). In other words, although Jesus's claim overrides the claim of family where there is a clash, it does not negate responsibility to love those entrusted to us. It can be a delicate balance, but Jesus's call on a person's life is absolute, just as God's is. There is no tension between Jesus calling someone to leave family and follow him and God's command to honor one's father and mother.

There is another dimension to Jesus's appointing the twelve in 3:14–15. Commentators agree that the number twelve represents Israel in some form but dispute the precise nature of the relationship between the twelve disciples and Israel. Do they represent the foundations of a "new" (i.e., replacement) Israel, or is there a stronger continuity between the nation and the twelve? I will take up this question in chapter 6, but for now I should note Jesus's authority in gathering a people to himself. He does more than collect followers. Whatever the precise relationship of the apostles to Israel, something epoch changing occurs as he calls his disciples.

The next calling scene involves Levi, a tax collector (2:14). Despised by the wider culture because of their complicity with the Romans, tax

---

12   Strauss, *Mark*, 83.

collectors were later assigned the same status as "thieves and murderers" and could not appear as a "judge or witness in court." They were even excluded from the synagogue.[13] Although these later attitudes are somewhat more extreme than in the New Testament, we see their origins here. When Jesus calls this tax collector to follow him and associates with his colleagues and other "sinners," the Pharisees respond with surprise (2:16). Jesus replies by affirming that he came "not to call the righteous, but sinners" (2:17).

It is tempting—and common—to view the twelve as inept and uncomprehending. This is not strictly accurate since the twelve also appear at different points as model disciples. The first half of Mark, in particular, is marked by notable success. For example, when Jesus sends out the twelve, "they went out and proclaimed that people should repent. And they cast out many demons and anointed with oil many who were sick and healed them" (6:12–13).

However, failures outnumber successes. They regularly fail to understand Jesus's teaching (e.g., 4:13), fail to believe (e.g., 4:40), and are said by Jesus to have hard hearts (8:17). Their failure to understand reaches a crescendo when Peter rebukes Jesus for speaking about his death (8:32). Peter's rebuke is met, in turn, with the most severe rebuttal: "Get behind me, Satan!" (8:33). This inability to grasp the necessity of Jesus's death persists throughout the Gospel (e.g., 9:32). However, their failure goes beyond misunderstanding: Judas betrays Jesus (3:19); Peter, James, and John sleep at Gethsemane (14:32–42); the disciples flee when Jesus is arrested (14:50); and Peter denies his master (14:67–72).

Why such a dismal, or at best mixed, presentation of the twelve? First, as we will see, the twelve are not the only characters who follow Jesus. The other, so-called minor, characters often respond well to Jesus—better than the twelve do. His disciples thus serve as a foil to the positive portrayals.

13 James R. Edwards, *The Gospel according to Mark*, PNTC (Grand Rapids, MI: Eerdmans, 2002), 83.

Second, remembering that Mark writes "the beginning of the gospel" sharpens our focus on the disciples' area of struggle: the cross and resurrection. Again, we see the overlap with Paul's insistence that the cross is the wisdom of God (1 Cor. 2:7). Without the cross we can understand neither God nor Christ, and we cannot follow the Lord Jesus rightly. However, the cross appears utterly foolish (1 Cor. 1:18, 21; 2:8) unless God reveals its significance to a person (1 Cor. 2:10). What Paul teaches in his letters, Mark displays in his narrative, demonstrating that even those closest to Jesus could not live the Christian life apart from the effects of the cross and resurrection.

Third, we nevertheless find hints of what the twelve (minus Judas) will become after the cross and resurrection. Despite his abrupt ending, Mark leads his readers to anticipate the risen Jesus's on-going relationship with the twelve (Mark 14:28; 16:7).[14] Their failure is not terminal. Perhaps the clearest indication of future transformation comes in Mark 13 where Jesus speaks about the gospel being "proclaimed to all nations" (13:10). Furthermore, in preparing them to one day stand trial, Jesus assumes they will be faithful to him and his words (13:11). They will not abandon the gospel as they had abandoned Jesus in his hour of need. Moreover, they need not be anxious concerning what to say: it will not be them speaking "but the Holy Spirit" (13:11).

References to the Holy Spirit are infrequent in Mark. The Spirit is present with Jesus at his baptism (1:10) and his temptation (1:12), and the Spirit is the subject of his confrontation with the scribes who attributed his miracles to an unclean spirit (3:29). Jesus also ascribes David's insight in Psalm 110:1 to the Holy Spirit (12:36). However, with respect to believers there are only two references: John the Baptist's prophecy that Jesus would baptize with the Holy Spirit (1:8) and the promise that it would not be the disciples who spoke but the Holy Spirit (13:11). While Mark does not present developed teaching on the Holy Spirit, he makes the subtle but clear point that the Spirit alone brings about the transformation in the disciples. To be baptized in the Spirit

14   Stein, *Mark*, 32.

(1:8) enables one to speak confidently before opponents of Jesus and the gospel (13:10)—the very thing that the disciples fail to do. As Mark writes for people who have heard the gospel and who know that understanding comes by the Spirit (cf. 1 Cor. 2:14), he shows what life without the Spirit looks like—it is suffused with failure and incomprehension.

Other Characters

Jesus rebukes the disciples for lacking faith (4:40), lacking understanding (8:21), and having hard hearts (8:17). Each of these is overcome by the Spirit's work following the cross and resurrection. However, Mark does not simply portray the pre-cross failure of Jesus's disciples. While that is the dominant note of his portrayal of the twelve (with some exceptions as we have seen), he presents a host of minor characters much more positively. They do understand and demonstrate faithful discipleship.

Helen Bond warns against leaning too heavily on minor characters to give coherence to Mark's narrative. Rather, "Mark's text achieves its unity . . . in a very different way: what links all of the episodes for our author is the central character, Jesus."[15] Moreover, "Mark's focus on Jesus is so all-pervading that other characters exist only to bring Jesus's *ēthos* and virtues into greater clarity."[16] As Whitney Shiner notes, "*Characters in Mark's Gospel serve primarily to further the portrayal of Jesus.*"[17] With these cautions in mind, we examine the minor characters not purely on their own terms but in relation to Jesus.

Jesus heals many of the minor characters, but not all are called to follow him. Jesus commands the *lepros* in 1:40–45 not to speak about what happened but to go and make an offering for cleansing as proof of his healing (1:44). Instead, the man "went out and began to talk freely," rendering Jesus unable to "openly enter a town" (1:45). The paralytic Jesus heals in 2:1–10 is commanded to "go home" (2:11). The formerly

---

15 Helen Bond, *The First Biography of Jesus: Genre and Meaning in Mark's Gospel* (Grand Rapids, MI: Eerdmans, 2020), 195.

16 Bond, *First Biography*, 195.

17 Whitney Shiner, *Follow Me! Disciples in Markan Rhetoric*, SBLDS 145 (Atlanta: Scholars, 1995), 8 (emphasis in original), cited in Bond, *First Biography*, 195.

demon-possessed man wanted to accompany Jesus, but Jesus instead sends him home to his friends to "tell them how much the Lord has done for you, and how he has had mercy on you" (5:18–19). The woman with the discharge of blood is told to "go in peace" (5:34). Jairus and his family are instructed to tell no one what had happened (5:43). Jesus tells the Syrophoenician woman, "You may go your way" (7:29). He commands the deaf man to remain silent about his healing (7:36). The blind man at Bethsaida is ordered to go straight home and not even to "enter the village" (8:26). The boy with the unclean spirit is healed, but neither he nor his father receive any instruction (9:14–29). The encounter with the rich man (not a healing) contains the challenge to sell everything he has and follow Jesus (10:21). The final suppliant in the Gospel is Bartimaeus, the blind man whom Jesus heals in Jericho. Having healed him, Jesus tells him to go his way, but instead he "followed him on the way" (10:52). We meet one more minor character, a woman with an alabaster jar of expensive perfume who anoints Jesus for his burial. Jesus tells the onlookers that "wherever the gospel is proclaimed in the whole world, what she has done will be told in memory of her" (14:9).

The variety of responses to which Jesus calls them underlines the point made earlier: following Jesus takes various forms. The call of the twelve—that is, leave everything and *physically* follow Jesus to the cross—differs from Jesus's instruction to others. We can, furthermore, extract other discipleship principles from these minor characters.

The female characters in particular embody what has been called "narrative discipleship." Jeffrey Aernie focusses on eight women in Mark: Simon's mother-in-law (1:29–31); the bleeding woman (5:25–34); the Syrophoenician woman (7:24–30); the poor widow (12:41–44); the woman who anoints Jesus (14:3–9); Mary Magdalene, Mary, and Salome in the passion narrative (15:40–41, 47; 16:1–8). He suggests that their stories should be read together and that their narratives "extend the theological framework in which the life of discipleship can be worked out."[18]

---

18   Jeffrey W. Aernie, *Narrative Discipleship: Patterns of Women in the Gospel of Mark* (Eugene, OR: Pickwick, 2018), 3.

Aernie argues that these women model the "essential characteristics of Markan discipleship"—namely, "restored life, kingdom speech, sacrificial action, and cruciformity."[19] So healing Simon's mother-in-law (1:29–31) essentially restores her to life, which translates to restored service: "she began to serve them" (1:31). The Syrophoenician woman is an example of "kingdom speech" in that her "importance rests in her ability to speak the reality of the gospel" (7:27–28).[20] "Active discipleship" appears in the poor widow's sacrifice at the temple (12:41–44) and in the woman who anoints Jesus (14:1–9). Finally, the women who remain as Jesus dies (albeit "looking on from a distance") exemplify "cruciformity" as they stay at the cross while the other disciples flee (15:40).[21]

Aernie's analysis is a helpful corrective to a narrow view of discipleship that only focuses on the twelve or on Jesus's teaching. He shows that discipleship even in Jesus's lifetime could take forms other than *physically* following him. The breadth of discipleship is also seen in Jesus's teaching on the topic.

Jesus's Teaching on Discipleship

Mark 8:34 recounts Jesus's most pointed teaching on the nature of discipleship. This instruction applies to all (i.e., not simply the twelve) who want to follow him and includes three elements:[22] denying oneself, taking up one's cross, and following him.

Mark narrates instances of each of the three elements, allowing us to see what they look like in practice. The first is perhaps the most radical. One must deny not "things that the self wants, but the self itself."[23] In 2 Timothy 2:13, Paul speaks about the impossibility of God denying himself, which would entail acting "contrary to his own nature, to cease to be God."[24] Calling his followers to do what is impossible for God,

19 Aernie, *Narrative Discipleship*, 3.
20 Aernie, *Narrative Discipleship*, 80.
21 Aernie, *Narrative Discipleship*, 83.
22 Schnabel, *Mark*, 202.
23 Schnabel, *Mark*, 202.
24 France, *Mark*, 340.

Jesus requires a "a radical abandonment of one's own identity and self-determination." They are to join the "march to the place of execution."[25]

The second element, to take up one's cross, is Mark's first reference to "cross" (*stauros*) and the only reference outside the passion narrative (Mark 15:21, 30, 32). It foreshadows the manner of Jesus's death and graphically illustrates the cost of following him—all the way to his death. A note of willingly sharing Jesus's shame is also present (cf. Heb. 12:2).[26] Although this summons includes a literal sense—that is, being willing to endure physical death—the breadth of discipleship experience in the Gospel suggests that it also includes the broader, metaphorical sense and "serves to reinforce and intensify what it means to deny oneself."[27]

The final requirement generates a circular statement: "If anyone wishes to follow after me . . . let him follow me."[28] The sense is that following Jesus must be an ongoing process.[29] Peter's claim that the disciples have "left everything and followed" Jesus (Mark 10:28) elicits a positive response (10:29–30). By the time that Jesus goes to the cross, however, Peter has abandoned him.

Jesus expands on his threefold call by providing reasons and consequences in 8:35–38. His paradoxical statement shows that this life of self-denying discipleship seems like loss of life but actually saves it. To deny Jesus's call to discipleship, to cling to one's life and avoid his summons to death, is really to lose one's life. "The one for whom the way of Jesus is more important than his own existence will secure his eternal being; but the one whose existence is more important than Jesus will lose both Jesus and his existence."[30]

Not to be overlooked is Jesus's insistence that his followers lose their life not just for his sake but also for the gospel's sake (8:35). Discipleship as imitation of Jesus finds its counterpoint in mission.[31]

25 France, *Mark*, 340.
26 Stein, *Mark*, 407.
27 Stein, *Mark*, 407.
28 My own translation.
29 Stein, *Mark*, 407.
30 Edwards, *Mark*, 257.
31 France, *Mark*, 341.

Cross-shaped discipleship, however paradoxical it might sound, is the way to life. In economic terms, gaining the whole world is worth nothing if it costs one's soul (8:36), and a person can give nothing to purchase his or her soul (8:37). That is, it is impossible to regain your soul once you have lost it.[32] Mark 8:38 moves from economics to eschatology as Jesus speaks of the end of the age and the coming of the Son of Man in glory. When he comes, Jesus will be ashamed of whoever has been ashamed of him and his words (cf. a reference to the gospel in 8:35) in "this adulterous and sinful generation."[33]

Jesus has moved from predicting his death to reflecting on a life of following him and carrying one's own cross. Mark illustrates this negatively and positively throughout his Gospel. The twelve model it negatively as Jesus's own death approaches. Rather than deny himself, Peter denies Jesus three times (14:30–31; 72). While the others do not deny him verbally, neither do they follow him to the cross. They, too, abandon him (14:50). However, we also find positive models in the two Marys and Salome, who remain with Jesus to the end, even if they watch the crucifixion "from a distance" (15:40).

This is not Jesus's only teaching concerning discipleship. We have seen that one of the most common titles applied to Jesus is "teacher." Significant teaching in the first half of the Gospel includes his parables (4:13–34), his clashes with the Pharisees and scribes over the nature of purity (7:1–23), and his warning to the disciples to avoid the leaven of the Pharisees and Herod (8:11–21). But the middle section of the Gospel—from when Jesus begins to teach on his death and resurrection (8:31) until he enters Jerusalem (11:1)—forms the most concentrated section of teaching. Mark 8:31–10:52 forms a coherent section of the Gospel as indicated by its framing with accounts of Jesus healing blind

---

32 So Strauss, *Mark*, 374.

33 Although in light of Dan. 7:13 this could be referring to the ascension (since it describes the coming of the Son of Man into the presence of the "Ancient of Days"—i.e., God), the mention of shame more naturally refers to his coming in judgment at the end of time. The various "comings" of the Son of Man can be tricky to relate. On their use in Matthew, see Ben Cooper, "Adaptive Eschatological Inference from the Gospel of Matthew," *JSNT* 33, no. 1 (2010): 59–80.

men (8:22–26; 10:46–52) and the repeated use of the phrase "on the way" (*en tē hodos* in 8:27; 9:33; 9:34; 10:32; 10:52).[34] As Jesus approaches Jerusalem, "the themes of self-sacrifice and willingness to serve become even stronger, even as Jesus's predictions of his impending death become even clearer."[35] He calls his disciples to give up everything—riches, homes, and families (10:17–22, 23–30).[36] Disciples are to be servants. In fact, "whoever would be great among you must be your servant, and whoever would be first among you must be slave of all" (10:43–44)—illustrated most powerfully in the life of Jesus himself who, as the Son of Man, came "not to be served but to serve, and to give his life as a ransom for many" (10:45). Jesus's countercultural teaching thus "is not simply a blueprint for others but forms the basis for how Jesus will conduct his own life."[37]

This central section is structured around Jesus's three passion predictions (8:31; 9:30; 10:33–34). The pattern of Jesus's first passion prediction repeats in the other two. Each is followed with teaching on the shape of discipleship—as it is exemplified in the narrative of the Gospel.[38] As Aernie points out, the disciples react negatively to Jesus's passion predictions with "insolence (8:32–33), fearful silence (9:32), and misplaced arrogance (10:35–41)."[39] However, in each case Jesus corrects their reaction by teaching on the nature of discipleship—"cruciformity (8:34–38), inversion of social hierarchies (9:35–37), and self-sacrificial service (10:42–45)."[40] Each failure to grasp the significance of Jesus's death proves that "a wrong view of Messiahship leads to a wrong view of discipleship."[41]

In the midst of this section about following Jesus to death, about selling everything one has to follow Jesus (10:21), about leaving family

---

34 Bond, *First Biography*, 151.
35 Bond, *First Biography*, 152.
36 Bond, *First Biography*, 152.
37 Bond, *First Biography*, 153.
38 Aernie, *Narrative Discipleship*, 32–33.
39 Aernie, *Narrative Discipleship*, 32.
40 Aernie, *Narrative Discipleship*, 32–33.
41 Edwards, *Mark*, 256.

for Jesus's sake and for the gospel (10:28), Jesus teaches that divorce opposes God's original intention for marriage (10:7–9) and that remarriage following divorce equates to adultery (10:10–12). As Mark Strauss notes, "Jesus's followers must not abandon difficult marriage relationships simply because they are not meeting their personal needs. Authentic discipleship is not about self-gratification, but about giving oneself in sacrificial service for the kingdom of God."[42] He also suggests that the whole section "connects to the passages before and after with the theme of God's love and concern for the lowest members of society, since in the ancient world women (10:5–9) and children (9:36–37, 42; 10:14–16) were among the most vulnerable to exploitation and abuse."[43] Furthermore, this passage *domesticates* (in the non-pejorative sense of this word) Jesus's radical teaching of 8:34–38. Following Jesus, denying oneself, and carrying the cross for Jesus's sake and for the gospel does not mean abandoning one's marriage or children.

In fact, discipleship means more than sacrifice—those who leave earthly ties will find them replaced "a hundredfold now in this time" and will receive "in the age to come eternal life" (10:30). The list of things abandoned for the sake of Jesus and the gospel is matched a hundredfold—except for one's father (since God is to be their only Father)[44]—with the addition of persecutions (10:29–30).

This teaching widens discipleship beyond the experience of the first disciples. For the twelve, discipleship meant literally following Jesus to his death. They failed utterly as all of them abandoned him and Peter denied him. But physically following Jesus to the cross is no longer possible. This change thus qualifies how we should apply the call to leave family (1:16–20) to contemporary discipleship. The call to discipleship, however, remains radical. It still contains the call to death, but this is expressed differently now that Jesus is no longer physically present.

Mark 9:38–41 anticipates the post-resurrection experience of discipleship. The disciples recount how they tried to stop someone casting

42 Strauss, *Mark*, 419.
43 Strauss, *Mark*, 419.
44 Edwards, *Mark*, 316n42.

out demons in Jesus's name because "he was not following us" (9:38). As Robert Stein wryly observes, "This may be the first time, but certainly not the last, in which ecclesiastical leaders have sought to hinder those who would minister in the name of Christ independently of their authority."[45] However, Jesus insists that no one who does a miracle in his name can speak against him, and then he lays down the principle, "The one who is not against us is for us" (9:40). He promises a reward for anyone who gives even a "cup of water" to one of the disciples because they "belong to Christ" (9:41). This last phrase is important. Jesus speaks not simply of "benevolence and charity" but of aiding his followers because "they belong to and work for Jesus the Messiah."[46] Supporting God's servants leads to reward.

Conclusion

Discipleship is central to Mark's Gospel. It is not disconected from Christology but rather "the proper outcome of a healthy christology."[47] The supreme example of discipleship in Mark is Jesus himself. He lives out and models the life of a disciple, and he does it to the end, serving others even to the point of death.[48]

We have seen both discipleship's radical nature—the call to follow Jesus unto death—and its domestic nature—the command to remain married unto death. This discipleship, while focused on following and making sacrifices for Jesus, is also "for the sake of the gospel" and therefore connects to mission. In fact, it reaches beyond following and imitating Jesus to participating in Jesus's own mission.

This theme runs through the Gospels—and, to an extent, Acts—but after that it largely falls away. The language of discipleship (*mathētēs* and *akoloutheō*) never appears outside these five books, but this does not mean that discipleship merely relates to Jesus's earthly ministry. The *concept* of discipleship continues, even if the language does not.

---

45 Stein, *Mark*, 446.
46 Schnabel, *Mark*, 226.
47 France, *Mark*, 28.
48 Stein, *Mark*, 33.

For example, Paul speaks of the imitation of Christ (1 Cor. 4:16; 11:1) and also of a life devoted to the "work of the Lord" (1 Cor. 15:58). Perhaps the clearest parallel to Jesus's central teaching on discipleship in Mark 8:34–38 appears in Paul's letter to the Galatians. He reflects on his relationship to Christ and to the world. He has been "crucified with Christ" and denies his own existence by stating, "It is no longer I who live." His life "in the flesh" is lived "by faith in the Son of God" (Gal. 2:20). Later he states that he only boasts "in the cross of our Lord Jesus Christ, by which the world has been crucified to me, and I to the world" (Gal. 6:14). The echoes with Jesus's teaching are compelling. Paul understands that the radical call of discipleship continues, even when the possibility of *physically* following Jesus no longer remains.[49]

Mark narrates what discipleship looks like without the cross, the resurrection, and the Spirit—ultimately, failure. The command to follow Jesus unto death cannot be carried out without his work on the cross and the gift of the Spirit. Mark also underlines the importance of women in the early church. Where the twelve so frequently fail, many of the minor characters succeed, and among these the women dominate, illustrating most effectively what it means to be a disciple of Jesus.

---

49 This point is developed by Troels Engberg-Pedersen, "Paul in Mark 8:34–9:1: Mark on What It Is to Be a Christian," in *Mark and Paul: Comparative Essays Part II: For and Against Pauline Influence on Mark*, ed. Eve-Marie Becker, Troels Engberg-Pedersen, and Mogens Müller, BZNW 199 (Berlin: De Gruyter, 2014), 189–209.

What Moses Commanded

Jesus, the Law, and the People of God

THROUGHOUT THIS BOOK I have sought to connect Mark's "beginning of the gospel" to other writings in the New Testament, particularly the letters of Paul. A frequent theme in Paul's letters is the law of Moses. How does a Christian relate to the law (obey it? fulfill it? ignore it?)? Another important theme for Paul is the makeup of God's people. How does the people of God, defined by the law in the Old Testament, change in the New Testament? These are important themes (the law and the people of God) in Paul and, as we will see, in Mark's Gospel too. Considering these two themes further clarifies how Mark writes in conversation with the theology of the apostle Paul in particular.

The place of the law of Moses and its impact on both the individual and the corporate people of God displays a certain complexity. Jesus tells the man he healed of a serious skin disease to go and "show yourself to the priest and offer for your cleansing what Moses commanded, for a proof to them" (Mark 1:44). In this, Jesus affirms the validity of the law. However, at different points—particularly with respect to the Sabbath, food laws, and marriage—Jesus seems to modify or even revoke the law. For example, in 2:23–3:8, Jesus's interpretation of the Sabbath, at the very least, differs from that of the Pharisees. In Mark 7, the Evangelist understands Jesus's teaching on food to mean that "he declared all foods clean" (7:19). While these cases present Jesus as relaxing the law of Moses (although we will see the reality is more complex than that), 10:1–12 present a tightening of the law with respect to marriage and divorce.

Related to these ethical questions concerning the law of Moses, Mark presents the issue of the people of God in relation to the law. Mark does not have any discussion on circumcision—a topic prevalent in Paul but not in the Gospels. However, Mark does explore the makeup of the people of God. Mark 1 opens with people from "all the country of Judea and all Jerusalem" going to John the Baptist (1:5) and ends with people "from every quarter" going to Jesus (1:45). Admittedly these would have been from Jewish regions, but the phrase "from every quarter" evokes the issue of the identity of the people of God—and it is noteworthy that this phrase occurs immediately after the man with *lepra* disobeys Jesus's instruction to go and offer "what Moses commanded" following his healing (1:44).

The Gospel, as it unfolds, both focuses and widens the identity of the people of God. Mark focuses the identity of God's people with the call of the twelve (3:13–19). He widens the identity with, for example, Jesus's encounter with the Syrophoenician woman (7:24), the promise of worldwide gospel proclamation (13:10), and the gathering of the elect from the four winds (13:27). The question of Israel's identity also hovers in the background: is Israel replaced, renewed, or redefined?

To discuss these issues, I will first consider the law of Moses and then Mark's understanding of the people of God. I will then examine how these two themes interact with each other and how Mark's teaching about them relates to the wider New Testament.

The Law of Moses

Ritual Impurity

The first reference to the law of Moses is Jesus commanding the man healed of *lepra* to go and make an offering in obedience to what Moses commanded (1:44). However, before considering this command, we need to more closely examine the interaction as a whole. When the *lepros* approaches Jesus, he falls before him saying, "If you will, you can make me clean" (1:40). Jesus's response in 1:41, according to the ESV, is that he was "moved with pity" (*splanchistheis*). However, according to the NIV, Jesus "was indignant" (*orgistheis*). These are not alternate translations of the same Greek word but differing opinions concerning the underlying Greek word since the earliest manuscripts vary.

I cannot offer a detailed discussion of this complex issue.[1] Suffice it to say that Mark probably wrote of Jesus's *indignation*. This is the harder reading and would more likely have been changed by a scribe to the easier reading that Jesus had compassion or pity on the man. Even if we considered "moved with pity" to be original, we have to ask why Jesus, after he healed the man, "sternly charged him and sent him away at once" (1:43).

Why would Jesus be indignant with a man for asking him to heal his *lepra*? With what exactly is he angry? Four possibilities emerge: the man himself, the disease, a demon believed to be connected to the disease, or the ritual purity system.[2]

Matthew Thiessen has given a recent, convincing treatment of this encounter. He rejects the idea that Jesus was angry at the ritual purity system since Jesus proceeds to *purify* this man, saying "be clean" (1:41).[3] Although some early Jewish and Christian texts connected *lepra* and the demonic, that is not the focus of Mark's account of the story. And in any case even after he cleanses the man, "Jesus continues his angry behavior—growling at the man and casting him away."[4] This last feature suggests that rather than being angry at the presence of the disease, he is angry or indignant with the man himself. But why would Jesus be angry with him? The man has demonstrated faith in Jesus.

---

1   External evidence (i.e., number and quality of manuscripts) favors *splanchistheis*, while internal evidence (as I argue here) favors *orgistheis*. See Matthew Thiessen, *Jesus and the Forces of Death: The Gospels' Portrayal of Ritual Impurity Within First-Century Judaism* (Grand Rapids, MI: Baker Academic, 2021), 55n42.

2   Thiessen gives more detail (*Jesus and the Forces of Death*, 57).

3   Thiessen, *Jesus and the Forces of Death*, 58.

4   Thiessen, *Jesus and the Forces of Death*, 59.

Jesus is probably angry because of the implied question behind the man's approach to him—that is, "You can heal me if you are willing. Are you willing?" Unlike the father of the demon-possessed boy who questions Jesus's *ability* to heal his son and earns a (mild) rebuke (9:22–23), here the issue is Jesus's *desire* to heal this man's *lepra*. This disease carries "such momentous consequence that Jesus desires to purify those who suffer from it, becoming angry at the thought that anyone would believe otherwise."[5]

Jesus's response highlights his *desire*: "I will; be clean" (1:41). He then sternly commands the man not to speak to anyone but to "offer for your cleansing what Moses commanded" (1:44). The reference is to Leviticus 14:1–8, which deals with the cleansing of a person with *lepra*. Thus, Thiessen argues, Jesus does not overturn or reject the purity laws. His command to go to the priest and make the offering is not a sign of the inability of the priest to offer healing but instead proves Jesus's conformity to them. Mark "emphasizes that Jesus's actions both conform to the legislation of Leviticus and demonstrate his commitment to the temple cult and ritual purity system."[6] Far from being "indifferent to ritual impurity," Jesus "wages war in Mark's Gospel against the sources of ritual impurity."[7]

Thiessen argues well for his understanding of this passage even though (as we will see below) some of the wider conclusions he draws are less convincing. Thiessen connects ritual impurity with death (following the work of Jacob Milgrom).[8] Consider 2 Kings 5:7, where the king of Israel is asked to cure Naaman of *lepra* and he responds, "Am I God, to kill and to make alive, that this man sends word to me to cure a man of his leprosy?" *Lepra* is death, but Jesus "overcomes the

---

5   Thiessen, *Jesus and the Forces of Death*, 60.

6   Thiessen, *Jesus and the Forces of Death*, 63.

7   Thiessen, *Jesus and the Forces of Death*, 63. Cf. R. T. France, *The Gospel of Mark: A Commentary on the Greek Text*, NIGTC (Grand Rapids, MI: Eerdmans, 2002), 119, who notes in passing Jesus's "lack of concern for ritual purity."

8   See Jacob Milgrom, "The Dynamics of Ritual Purity in the Priestly System," in *Purity and Holiness: The Heritage of Leviticus*, ed. Marcel J. H. H. Poorthius and Joshua Schwartz, Jewish and Christian Perspectives Series 2 (Leiden: Brill, 2000), 29–32.

forces of impurity and ultimately death itself on the cross."[9] He defeats impurity-death with his own death. However, until that time he keeps the laws related to purity.

Sabbath

Mark 2:23–28 describes the first of Jesus's controversies with the Jewish leaders (here the Pharisees) over the Sabbath. The Pharisees observe Jesus walking through a grainfield and his disciples plucking ears of grain. They object, not because the disciples were plucking someone else's grain since this was specifically allowed in the law (Deut. 23:25) but because they were working on the Sabbath, which the fourth commandment forbade (Ex. 20:10). In fact, it was a capital offense (Ex. 31:14; cf. Num. 15:32–36). The law, however, did not give a *detailed* description of what actually constituted work. Later rabbinic writings did, and they specified reaping.[10] An argument can be made that these later decisions reflect earlier views, including the views of Jesus's opponents.

Jesus could have insisted that what his disciples were doing was not actually work and that plucking a few ears of grain was within the boundaries of the law. However, he chooses another approach. His argument at first blush seems obscure. He appeals to an incident in the life of David that seems to have no connection with the Sabbath. He recounts from 1 Samuel 21:1–6 David's expedition to Nob when, following a discussion with Ahimelech the priest, he "ate the bread of the Presence, which it is not lawful for any but the priests to eat, and also gave it to those who were with him" (Mark 2:26).

Jesus's argument has been variously interpreted.[11] Maybe Jesus points to an Old Testament example where in response to human need—hunger in both this and David's case—ritual law can be broken. However, Jesus's conclusion does not support this reading. It seems more likely

---

9 Thiessen, *Jesus and the Forces of Death*, 184.

10 See Mark L. Strauss, *Mark*, ZECNT (Grand Rapids, MI: Zondervan Academic, 2014), 145.

11 See Robert H. Stein, *Mark*, BECNT (Grand Rapids, MI: Baker Academic, 2008), 147, for a good summary.

that, given David's freedom in certain conditions to go against the law, Jesus, the authoritative Son of Man, has an even greater freedom to do so. This stands because "the Son of Man is lord even of the Sabbath" (2:28). But what of the intervening verse where Jesus states that the "Sabbath was made for man, not man for the Sabbath" (2:27)? How does it relate to the argument that if David could suspend the law, much more could Jesus?

Jesus makes two observations. The first is a statement about the true nature of the Sabbath: it is not meant to be a burden but was given to people for their good. The second is that as Son of Man he is the Lord of the Sabbath. Some argue that Mark has inserted this explanatory sentence (i.e., that the quotation marks—which are not original anyway—end after 2:27). However, the term "Son of Man" so consistently appears throughout Mark's Gospel as Jesus's way of referring to himself that it would be odd to attribute it to Mark in this case. Others suggest that Son of Man here simply means human—that is, the point is an extension of 2:27— the Sabbath is for humans because they are *lords* of the Sabbath. However, again, the use of the construction in the singular ("Son of Man" not "sons of man"), the fact that everywhere else in Mark it refers to Jesus, and the presence of the article in Greek (*the* Son of Man) all point to the more traditional understanding: Jesus refers to himself as the Lord of the Sabbath.

Thus, Jesus accomplishes two things in relationship to the law of Moses. First, he asserts his own authority *over* the law. But second, he asserts this authority not out of selfishness or rebellion but to meet human need—fulfilling the very purpose of the Sabbath. Jesus avoids "the extremes of both legalism and antinomianism."[12] The law is not regarded as "autonomous revelation, which in legalism tends to replace the person of God," nor is "Jesus a free agent who abrogates the Sabbath or the moral order or the revealed will of God, as in antinomianism."[13] Rather, Jesus's answer teaches "that the righteous purpose of God as

---

12 James R. Edwards, *The Gospel according to Mark*, PNTC (Grand Rapids, MI: Eerdmans, 2002), 97.

13 Edwards, *Mark*, 97.

manifested in the Torah can be recovered and fulfilled only in relation to Jesus, who is its Lord."[14]

The second Sabbath controversy (3:1–6) raises the stakes. Jesus heals a man with a withered hand while the Pharisees and the Herodians (their natural enemies) conspire to kill him. This is not Jesus's first healing on a Sabbath. In 1:21–28 he healed a man with an unclean spirit in a synagogue on the Sabbath. That healing was met with astonishment; this one with opposition.

In 3:1 Jesus enters a synagogue where he finds a man with a withered hand. Mark tells us, "They watched Jesus to see whether he would heal on the Sabbath, so that they might accuse him" (3:2). Later rabbinic opinion (which again might have reflected opinions of Jesus's day) was that "anything done with the intention of healing is defined as work, even if the same activity done without the intention of healing would not be classified as work."[15]

Again, rather than debate what constitutes legitimate work on the Sabbath, Jesus raises broader issues: "Is it lawful on the Sabbath to do good or to do harm, to save life or to kill?" (3:4). This man's life was not in danger, and not healing him would do no harm; but as I argued in chapter 4, doing good and saving life ultimately means reversing the effects of the fall.[16]

The Pharisees' response is instructive in two ways. First, Jesus meets their silence "with anger, grieved at their hardness of heart" (3:5). Hard hearts are especially significant in Mark (even used of the disciples in 6:52 and 8:17). Then, following Jesus's healing of the man, the Pharisees and Herodians plot to kill Jesus (3:9)—a clear instance of irony, given Jesus's question in 3:4 about saving life or killing.[17]

Although this second controversy does not generate a statement such as 2:28 ("the Son of Man is lord even of the Sabbath"), the issue

14 Edwards, *Mark*, 97.
15 Adela Yarbro Collins, *Mark: A Commentary on the Gospel of Mark*, Hermeneia (Minneapolis: Fortress, 2007), 207.
16 Stein, *Mark*, 155.
17 Stein, *Mark*, 156.

is similar. That is, the question is not primarily what is lawful on the Sabbath but whether Jesus, the Son of Man and Lord of the Sabbath, has the authority to do good and to heal on the Sabbath.[18] The answer, Mark demonstrates, is yes.

What we see in both of these controversies is that Jesus upholds the intent of the Sabbath command but not in a way that trumps the rest of Scripture. He does not simply overturn the law of Moses at this point but authoritatively interprets its true intention.

Food

Perhaps the most important, if not cryptic, passage concerning Jesus's relationship to the law of Moses is 2:18–22. Jesus replies to the people's observation that, unlike the disciples of the Pharisees and of John the Baptist, his disciples do not fast. Fasting was practiced in the Old Testament period although it was not a central feature of Old Testament law.[19] Some fasted to gain God's favor (e.g., 2 Sam. 12:15–23), and some in the context of war (1 Sam. 14:24–30). Zechariah 7:1–7 describes the tradition of fasting in memory of the temple's destruction. The call for the people to afflict themselves in the context of the Day of Atonement (Lev. 16:29, 31) probably included fasting. Collins notes that fasting became more frequent in the Second Temple period, indicating devotion, and she observes Suetonius's reference to Jewish fasting, suggesting that it was widespread and common enough for Roman writers to be aware of.[20]

Despite the widespread practice, Jesus's disciples do not fast. However, the reason Jesus gives for their non-fasting is most intriguing. He replies, "Can the wedding guests fast while the bridegroom is with them? As long as they have the bridegroom with them, they cannot fast. The days will come when the bridegroom is taken away from them, and then they will fast in that day" (Mark 2:19–20). Jesus's reference to himself as the bridegroom points, as I argued in chapter 1, to his

---

18 Stein, *Mark,* 155.
19 The following examples are from Collins, *Mark,* 198.
20 Collins, *Mark,* 198.

divine identity. As with the Sabbath encounters, Jesus's authoritative identity explains his and his disciples' conduct. In addition, Jesus's presence implies celebration. Fasting now—associated as it is with mourning—would be utterly inappropriate. Jesus speaks about the bridegroom being taken away, the first indication of his death in Mark, when it will be appropriate to fast.

These ideas are extended in Jesus's following metaphors: cloths on garments and wine in wineskins (2:21–22). In both cases he reasons that you can't mix old and new: you can't put a new patch on an old garment or new wine in an old wineskin. These parables are elusive, but their intent is clear—you cannot contain Jesus within the existing structures. He shines a light not on the law or the Old Testament but on the traditions of the Pharisees—their practices of fasting add to the Old Testament law rather than obey it. As Jesus says, "New wine is for fresh wineskins" (2:22).

Another controversy concerning food arises in Mark 7:1–13. Jesus rebukes the Pharisees for disobeying the commandment to honor their parents in order to express their greater devotion to God, thus "making void the word of God" (7:13). This dispute is in the context of Jesus's disciples not following the tradition of the elders in ceremonially washing their hands before they eat. However, Jesus does not debate the relative value of tradition versus the word of God (in this case, the law of Moses). He teaches that external things going into the body (e.g., food eaten with unclean hands) do not defile a person; rather, sinful things that emerge from within make a person unclean (7:14–23). The corollary, as Mark states it, is that Jesus thus "declared all foods clean" (7:19). The length of this debate with the Pharisees and scribes shows its importance. At twenty-three verses, this is the longest dialogue between Jesus and his opponents in the book. According to Mark, Jesus's teaching overturns the clear statements of the law of Moses that certain foods were unclean (e.g., Lev. 11:2–47).

Some commentators point out the tension inherent in criticizing the Pharisees for breaking one part of the law (the fifth commandment) but then teaching that it is permissible to break another part (eating unclean food). As such they suggest that the aside in Mark 7:19 ("cleansing all the foods"[21]) was either added later or reflects Mark's theology rather than Jesus's own teaching. However, the textual evidence suggests that this saying is original. Moreover, to create a disjunction between Mark and Jesus at this point just shifts the problem. We would then have to ask why *Mark* sees no problem with the tension. Alternatively, Thiessen and others have argued that rather then declaring unclean food to be clean, Jesus instead declares that *clean* (kosher) food remains clean even if eaten with ritually unclean hands.[22]

Nevertheless, this reading fails to give proper weight to Jesus's teaching about impurity: it comes from *inside* a person not *outside*. "There is nothing outside a person that by going into him can defile him, but the things that come out of a person are what defile him" (7:15). Jesus insists that that "*whatever* [*pan*] goes into a person from outside cannot defile him" (7:18). Yes, the issue under discussion is eating with ritually unclean hands, but the scope of Jesus's pronouncement lifts the issue to another plane. As he continues, he *relativizes* ritual purity by teaching that internal sin defiles a person. In 7:21–22 he lists the sins that come "from within, out of the heart" and concludes that these "evil things come from within, and they defile a person" (7:23).

It is important to note the different time horizons in the passage: Jesus's interaction with the Pharisees, his later private instruction with the disciples, and Mark's still later editorial comment. Although 7:1–23 is concerned with Jesus's debate with the Pharisees, the instruction about the internal nature of defiling sin occurs after he has withdrawn in private with his disciples (7:17). The private teaching corresponds with what he has said to the people in 7:14–15 but is not directed to the Pharisees. Jesus explains to the disciples where true defilement comes from (with the implication that all food is now clean).

Mark's additional comment comes later still, when he writes "the beginning of the gospel." His Gospel is written after the proclamation

---

21 My translation.
22 Thiessen, *Jesus and the Forces of Death*, 194–95.

of the gospel to the Gentiles, after Peter's vision (Acts 10–11), and after the council of Jerusalem (Acts 15). Whether or not Mark writes with an eye to these events is beside the point. We can, however, say that he was writing into a church context where these issues were contentious. The reflections in Romans 14 (e.g., Rom. 14:20: "everything is indeed clean") and 1 Corinthians 8 show that debates about diet endured.

As well as noting the temporal horizons of the passage, we need to recognize Jesus's authority as presented by Mark. Jesus's pronouncement reflects his status "as the Messiah and Son of God (Mark 1:1) who proclaims the new reality of the kingdom of God in which food no longer defiles a person, taking his followers back to the time before Moses when all food was clean."[23] As we will see below with marriage, rather than overturn Torah, Jesus returns it to its true intention.

Marriage

Before turning to Jesus's teaching concerning marriage, divorce, and his own relationship to the law of Moses, we need to briefly consider John the Baptist's encounter with Herod (Mark 6:14–29). John dies for opposing Herod's marriage to his brother's wife, which was unlawful. Although Deuteronomy 25:5–10 permitted (required even) a man to marry his brother's widow to continue his line, in cases where (presumably) there already were children, Leviticus 18:16 prohibited a man from marrying his brother's widow. This latter verse was understood to imply, as was the case with Herod, that marrying your sister-in-law while your brother was still alive was also forbidden. Mark presents John as a righteous prophet, and his defense of the law of Moses is part of that portrayal. The narrative thus supplies a positive example of someone upholding the law of Moses regarding marriage.

Jesus's own teaching on marriage appears in Mark 10. When asked by the Pharisees whether it is "lawful for a man to divorce his wife," Jesus responds by asking what Moses *commanded* (10:3–4). By his question,

---

23 Eckhard J. Schnabel, *Mark: An Introduction and Commentary*, TNTC (Downers Grove, IL: IVP Academic, 2017), 169.

Jesus may be challenging them to realize (as he is about to argue) that while Moses *permitted* divorce, he did not actually *command* it. Or he may be inviting them to distinguish between what God commands and permits.[24] In any case, as Jesus continues, he reminds the Pharisees that divorce was only a concession—it was never God's intention for marriage. Jesus points to God's original intention for marriage: "A man shall leave his father and mother and hold fast to his wife, and the two shall become one flesh" (Mark 10:7–8, quoting Gen. 2:24). Jesus continues, "So they are no longer two but one flesh. What therefore God has joined together, let not man separate" (Mark 10:8–9). The Pharisees had observed that Moses permitted "a man to write a certificate of divorce and to send" his wife away (10:4, pointing to Deut. 24:1–4). Jesus replies that this stemmed from their "hardness of heart" and actually opposed God's original intention (Mark 10:5–6). Therefore, in light of Genesis 2, Jesus equates divorce and remarriage with adultery during his subsequent private conversation with the disciples (Mark 10:11–12).

Jesus's teaching on divorce in Mark 10 parallels his teaching on purity in Mark 7. Some have argued that the traditional reading of Mark 7 (defended above), which argues that Jesus declared *all* food clean (not just *kosher* food eaten with ritually unclean hands), would be "the only instance among the four gospels where Jesus is portrayed rejecting Torah."[25] However, in Mark 10, Jesus explicitly overturns Moses's teaching in Deuteronomy 24:1–4; it has been rejected. Jesus has gone back to the original intention of creation in Genesis 2. This resembles Jesus's teaching concerning the food laws: he reestablishes the situation after the flood when God tells Noah, "Every moving thing that lives shall be food for you" (Gen. 9:3).

Jesus even points to a time when marriage itself will no longer be practiced. In the discussion with the Sadducees regarding the woman who had seven husbands, Jesus replies that "when they rise from the

---

24 Both of these suggestions are considered by Strauss, *Mark*, 423–24.

25 John van Maaren, "Does Mark's Jesus Abrogate Torah? Jesus' Purity Logion and Its Illustration in Mark 7:15-23," *Journal of the Jesus Movement in its Jewish Setting* 4 (2017): 25.

dead, they neither marry nor are given in marriage, but are like angels in heaven" (Mark 12:25). There is a time to come, then, beyond the scope of the Mosaic law.

Although the temporal argument in Mark 10 is less explicit than in Mark 7, the result is the same. A law that was specific to Israel (permissible divorce; cf. restricted food in Mark 7) is set aside for the more fundamental, earlier command that God had laid down. Thus, as with the food laws, Jesus is not so much overturning the Mosaic law as he is reaching beyond it to God's original intention. Mark essentially makes the argument that Paul makes in Galatians 3:17–26: the law was a temporary "guardian until Christ came" (Gal. 3:24).

The People of God

Because the man healed of *lepra* began to speak freely, Jesus could no longer move about freely, but people came to him "from every quarter [*pantōthen*]" (Mark 1:45). At the beginning of the Gospel, we see Jesus's universal appeal. This raises a question that bubbles away through much of the New Testament: what is the relationship between Jesus's disciples and Israel? More directly, is Israel being replaced or renewed?

The word "Israel" only appears twice in the Gospel. When someone asks Jesus to identify the most important command, he replies with the words of the Shema, "Hear, O Israel: The Lord our God, the Lord is one. And you shall love the Lord your God with all your heart and with all your soul and with all your mind and with all your strength" (12:29–30). Then when Jesus is crucified, the chief priests and scribes mock him: "Let the Christ, the King of Israel, come down now from the cross that we may see and believe" (15:32; cf. the references to "King of the Jews" in 15:2, 9, 12, 18, 26).

The scarcity of the term "Israel" is offset by Jesus's calling of the twelve (3:13–19). The number twelve points clearly to the tribes of Israel and indicates "that Jesus viewed himself, in some sense at least, as restoring, reforming, or reconstituting the remnant of Israel."[26] Moreover, the fact

---

26 Strauss, *Mark*, 159.

that Jesus did not identify himself as one of the twelve suggests that he "presents himself in the position of Yahweh, who created and elected Israel as his covenant people."[27]

This new Israel is configured around Jesus's call (3:13) and appointment (3:16) of the twelve. A parallel configuring occurs as Jesus interacts with his family. Hearing that they are outside, Jesus, looking at those who are seated around him, declares that "whoever does the will of God, he is my brother and sister and mother" (3:35). Jesus's family is reconstituted—not along physical lines but in terms of obedience to God's will. Similar things are happening with Israel. Ethnic Israel is not being shut out or excluded per se, but their *physical* relationship with Christ is not enough. Nothing prevented Jesus's physical family from obeying the will of God and becoming his true family (which did happen according to Acts 1:13). So nothing stopped *ethnic* Israel from following Jesus (as the twelve and others were doing) and becoming part of this reconstituted Israel.

One element that at first glance portrays ethnic Israel negatively is the parable of the vineyard and the tenants. This parable speaks of wicked tenants who hold back the vineyard's fruit from its owner. He sends a series of servants who are beaten and even killed. In a climactic attempt to recover his own fruit, the vineyard owner sends his son, saying to himself, "They will respect my son" (Mark 12:6). However, inevitably, the tenants seize and kill him too, thinking they will thereby gain ownership of the vineyard. As the parable concludes, Jesus describes the owner's reaction to the wicked tenants: "What will the owner of the vineyard do? He will come and destroy the tenants and give the vineyard to others" (12:9). Some have suggested that this parable speaks of the *replacement* of Israel by the church.[28] Instead, it seems that the *leadership* of God's people (the vineyard) is in view.[29] This leadership will be given to others. Already in Mark these leaders have been identified as the *Jewish*

---

27 Strauss, *Mark*, 159.
28 E.g., France, *Mark*, 462.
29 Strauss, *Mark*, 517.

apostles (3:13–19), even if the new leadership will eventually become predominantly Gentile.[30]

Furthermore, Jesus clearly anticipates Gentile inclusion in the new people of God. Indeed the gospel will be proclaimed "in the whole world" (14:9) and "to all nations" (13:10). However, Jesus's encounter with the Syrophoenician woman (7:25–30) underscores the priority of Israel in Jesus's ministry. The movement to the nations is a future reality. She begs Jesus to heal her daughter, only to hear: "Let the children be fed first, for it is not right to take the children's bread and throw it to the dogs" (7:27). The fact that she persuades Jesus to heal her daughter (7:28) suggests to some this response changed Jesus's mind with regard to the mission to the Gentiles.[31]

However, as others have shown, Jesus's response doesn't indicate a change of mind. Instead, his goal is to elicit faith from the woman. In fact, Jesus has already initiated a mission into Gentile territory. In 4:35, Jesus leads his disciples to the other side of the lake. That night Jesus calms a storm before arriving at the "country of the Gerasenes" (5:1). In this foreign region he encounters the man who could not be chained, and Jesus casts out the legion of spirits into a herd of pigs. Although a number of commentators downplay the Gentile character of this engagement, Garland underlines its significance: "In crossing the lake to an area where swine are kept, Jesus embarks on a daring invasion to claim alien turf under enemy occupation and reveals that there is no place in the world that God's reign does not intend to exert itself."[32]

In other words, the notion that the Syrophoenician woman changes Jesus's mind regarding the appropriateness of God's blessing going to

---

30 Morna D. Hooker, *The Gospel according to Saint Mark*, BNTC (London: Continuum, 1991), 276.

31 On this question see Matthew Malcolm, "Did the Syrophoenician Woman Change Jesus's Mission?," *BBR* 29, no. 2 (2019): 174–86.

32 David E. Garland, *A Theology of Mark's Gospel: Good News about Jesus the Messiah, the Son of God*, Biblical Theology of the New Testament (Grand Rapids, MI: Zondervan Academic, 2015), 273. This is the position Malcolm argues for in "Did the Syrophoenician Woman Change Jesus's Mission?," an interpretation that goes back as far as John Chrysostom.

foreigners fails because it overlooks the fact that he had already engaged in Gentile mission and in a particularly dramatic way.

Let's return to the question I asked earlier: Is Israel as the people of God being replaced, renewed, or redefined? The answer seems to be yes! Israel is not being replaced *as Israel*, but the locus of the people of God is no longer coterminous with Israel—the people of God will include Gentiles. This does not rule out an ongoing existence for Israel, although this is not Mark's primary concern (cf. Rom. 9–11). Furthermore, the "people of God" is being redefined, and if redefined then renewed. It is being reconstituted around the twelve and defined not in ethnic terms but in terms of relationship to Jesus.

Conclusion

The law of Moses and the people of God are not static entities. In fact, they never were. Laws on food changed: from Genesis 3:18 ("you shall eat the plants of the field") to 9:3 ("every moving thing that lives shall be food for you") to Leviticus 11 (only clean animals may be eaten). Now, in light of his coming, the kingdom's dawning, and his teaching that defilement comes from within, Jesus declares all foods clean (7:19), taking the situation back to a time before the law was given. A similar argument is made with respect to marriage and divorce. The law permitted divorce, but only because people's hearts were hard. This must no longer be the case—divorce is prohibited for a follower of Jesus.[33] He has restored marriage to its original, lifelong intention. However, in the future, there will be another change: marriage itself will be done away with.

By instituting such changes—even while acknowledging some continuity (e.g., he commands a sacrifice of cleansing to be made)—and by his Sabbath interactions, Jesus shows himself to be the authoritative teacher of Israel, the new Moses, the true lawgiver.

The makeup of the people of God, furthermore, reveals Jesus's divine role. Rather than participating in the new people of God, he forms

---

33 Matthew 19:9 indicates that this prohibition may not be absolute.

it, thus taking the role that God himself plays in the Old Testament. Although the focus in Mark (as in each of the Gospels) is on Jesus's ministry to Israel, inclusion in the people of God is redefined—even to the point of including the nations (13:10).

Here is another area where Mark and Paul overlap. Paul says much about the relevance of the law for the Christian life and about the relationship of Jew and Gentile in the people of God. For Paul, as for Mark, the change in redemptive history brought about by the death and resurrection of Jesus means that the Christian's relationship to the law differs from that of Israel under the law (e.g., Rom. 7:4–6; Gal. 3:24–25). With the death of Jesus, there is "neither Jew nor Greek" since we "are all one in Christ Jesus" (Gal. 3:28).

Died, Buried, and Raised

The Death and Resurrection of Jesus

TWO ASSERTIONS ARE OFTEN MADE about Mark's Gospel. First, it is essentially a "passion narrative with an extended introduction."[1] Second, it has no theology of atonement.[2] The first assertion is overstated; the second is incorrect. However, we are left to ask *why* Mark tells us so much about the death of Jesus. If gospel truth reduces to "Christ died for our sins in accordance with the Scriptures" (1 Cor. 15:3), what remains to be said? To answer this question, I will examine passages that narrate Jesus's suffering, and I will also penetrate the substructure of Mark's argument. This will tell us *why* he thinks the death of Jesus is so important. The final section will deal with the resurrection of Jesus.

Jesus's Death Foreshadowed

Even before Jesus enters Jerusalem, the shadow of the cross falls across the whole of the Gospel. Jesus himself makes three passion predictions

---

1 Martin Kähler, *The So-Called Historical Jesus and the Historic Biblical Christ*, trans. Carl E. Braaten (Philadelphia: Fortress, 1964), 80n11.

2 E.g., Cilliers Breytenbach, "Narrating the Death of Jesus in Mark: Utterances of the Main Character, Jesus," *ZNW* 105, no. 2 (2014): 162: "There are no indications in the Greek text of Mark suggesting the use of categories like 'atonement.'"

(Mark 8:31; 9:30–32; 10:33–34), which I will examine below. But as early as the first chapter, there are prefigurations of Jesus's death.

At Jesus's baptism (1:11) and again at his transfiguration (9:7), God identifies Jesus as his "beloved Son" (*ho huios mou ho agapētos*). I have already touched on how this alludes to Genesis 22:2 (LXX), where God tells Abraham to take "your beloved son whom you love"[3] (*ton huion sou ton agapēton*) and to offer him as a burnt offering on Mount Moriah. The allusion, if intended by Mark, points to Jesus's sacrificial death as God's beloved Son. Admittedly the allusion is subtle, but two things stand in its favor. First, Paul seems to make a connection between Isaac and Jesus in Romans 8:32 when he describes God as the one "who did not spare his own Son but gave him up for us all." Indeed, post-apostolic writers make this connection explicit. For example, the Epistle of Barnabas indicates that Jesus's death as a "sacrifice for our sins" was so that "the type established in Isaac when he was offered upon the altar might be brought to completion" (Barn. 7:3).[4] Second, later in Mark, in the parable of the tenants, the son who is killed by tenants and thrown out of the vineyard is described by Jesus as the "beloved son" of the owner of the vineyard (Mark 12:6). The phrase seems to prefigure Jesus's own death as God's beloved Son.

In 2:18–22 people ask Jesus why his disciples do not fast. Jesus answers that one does not fast while the bridegroom is present, but there will come a time "when the bridegroom is taken away from them" and then they will fast (2:20). The word for "taken away" (*apairō*) occurs only here and in the parallel passages in Matthew 9:15 and Luke 5:35. Being "taken away" could refer to the ascension, as Luke uses a cognate verb when he refers to this event in Acts 1:9 (*epairō*), but in this context fasting suggests mourning, which naturally evokes death. The LXX of Isaiah 53:8 describes the servant's life as "taken from the earth,"[5] the verb being another cognate: *airō*.[6] This possible connection with Isaiah 53

---

3   My translation.
4   My translation.
5   My translation.
6   Mark L. Strauss, *Mark*, ZECNT (Grand Rapids, MI: Zondervan Academic, 2014), 149.

hints at the *purpose* of Jesus's being "taken away"—a substitutionary death for the sins of others.

As the story unfolds, Jesus's conflict with the authorities intensifies, increasingly foreshadowing his death. Following the debate in the synagogue over the appropriateness of healing on the Sabbath, Mark relates that the Pharisees and Herodians conspired against Jesus, discussing how they might "destroy him" (Mark 3:6).

In the chapter that names the twelve, Judas is already identified as the one who "betrayed him" (3:19). This phrase suggests that Mark writes for those who know how the story ends. His description of Judas is the ultimate spoiler. Second, the verb translated "betrayed" (*paradidōmi*) is elsewhere translated "delivered over/up" (9:31; 10:33; 13:9, 11, 12; 15:1, 10, 15). Already Mark has used it in 1:14 to speak of John the Baptist's arrest. The word then adds to Judas's act of treachery the notion that he betrays him *to* others. Jesus will be delivered "into the hands of men" (9:31), more specifically "to the chief priests and the scribes," who in turn "deliver him over to the Gentiles" (10:33). Mark also tells us that Jesus was given over "into the hands of sinners" (14:41), to Pilate (15:1), and "to be crucified" (15:15). The same verb occurs in Isaiah 53, which states that the Lord "handed [the servant] over to our sins" (Isa. 53:6) and that the servant was "handed over to death" and "handed over because of their sins" (Isa. 53:12).[7]

The details of the text slowly accumulate to point to a violent death that resonates with the brutal, sin-bearing death of the servant in Isaiah 53. The violent nature of his death is further foreshadowed in Mark 6:14–28 and the demise of John the Baptist. Although this account primarily serves to contrast Herod (weak, murderous) with Jesus in the following passage of feeding the five thousand (authoritative, generous), the parallels that have already been drawn between John and Jesus (they both preach a message of repentance; 1:4, 14, etc.) suggest that the same kind of violent death awaits Jesus.

---

7   My translations.

Thus, long before reaching Jesus's passion predictions, Mark unveils the violent nature and even atoning significance of Jesus's death. And Jesus's own teaching on his death only intensifies the focus.

Jesus's Death Predicted

Following Peter's confession of Jesus as the Christ, Jesus commands the disciples not to make his identity known (8:29–30). He then instructs them that "the Son of Man must suffer many things and be rejected by the elders and the chief priests and the scribes and be killed, and after three days rise again" (8:31). He stresses the *necessity* of his death: the Son of Man "must" be killed. As we will see, this necessity arises from the Scriptures. If they are to be fulfilled and God's purposes realized, Jesus must die.

This first passion prediction also emphasizes the role of the Jewish leaders in Jesus's death. He will die at the hands of the elders, the chief priests, and the scribes. He will "suffer many things"—which is expanded in the third prediction to include mocking, spitting, and flogging (10:34). He will be "rejected," perhaps alluding to Psalm 118:22 ("the stone that the builders rejected"), a verse quoted at the end of Jesus's parable of the tenants (12:10).[8] Three days after being killed, he will rise again. Following Peter's rebuke of Jesus and Jesus's sharp retort (8:32–33), Jesus teaches on the nature of discipleship. Following him involves taking up (*airō*) one's cross (8:34). This is the first reference to "the cross" in Mark and anticipates the mode of Jesus's execution.

The second prediction is the simplest: Jesus, the Son of Man, will be delivered "into the hands of men" (9:31). He says nothing more about these men except that "they will kill him" and, again, that "after three days he will rise." The people directly responsible for Jesus's death have been identified in 8:31, but Jesus now speaks merely of "men," which underscores the "culpability of all humanity."[9] There may also be a note of irony, for the authoritative, sovereign Son of *Man* (see Dan. 7:13–14)

---

8   Strauss, *Mark*, 363.
9   Robert H. Stein, *Mark*, BECNT (Grand Rapids, MI: Baker Academic, 2008), 440.

is handed over to *men*. Furthermore, the fact that he is delivered (passive) into the hands of men may hint at the divine role in his being handed over. God is the one, Paul tells us, who delivered over his own Son for us (Rom. 4:25; 8:32).[10] So it is in Mark as well.

The final prediction (10:33–34) is expansive. Here Jesus reminds the disciples that they are going to Jerusalem. His death will happen in the religious capital of the nation. He will be "delivered over" to the Jewish leaders ("the chief priests and the scribes") who will "condemn him to death." The legal language of "condemn" (*katakrinō*) points to Jesus's trial, after which the leaders will "deliver him over to the Gentiles" (10:33). Jesus describes the horrors of his suffering: the Gentiles will "mock him and spit on him, and flog him" before they kill him. "And after three days he will rise" (10:34).

Following this third prediction, Jesus again instructs his disciples concerning the nature of discipleship. James and John ask Jesus that they may sit at his right and left in his "glory" (10:37). Jesus asks them, "Are you able to drink the cup that I drink, or to be baptized with the baptism with which I am baptized?" (10:38). Both metaphors refer to his death. The baptism, it is generally agreed, points to the violent nature of his death. The background to the imagery is found in the idea that suffering is "an overwhelming deluge" (e.g., Isa. 43:2).[11] The cup portrays God's wrath. Isaiah 51:17 refers to the "cup of his wrath" as punishment that Jerusalem will have to drink. These two images indicate how Jesus in his death will be overwhelmed with the wrath of God.

The first and third passion predictions, then, are followed by instruction on the nature of discipleship that, in turn, reveals something specific about the nature of Jesus's death—on a cross (Mark 8:34) and bearing the wrath of God (10:38).

These are generally identified as the three formal passion predictions in the Gospel of Mark, but when Jesus descends with the disciples from the Mount of Transfiguration, they ask about Elijah. While explaining

10   Strauss, *Mark*, 407.

11   Eckhard J. Schnabel, *Mark: An Introduction and Commentary*, TNTC (Downers Grove, IL: IVP Academic, 2017), 251.

that Elijah's coming is fulfilled in the life of John the Baptist, Jesus points to the fact that "it is written of the Son of Man that he should suffer many things and be treated with contempt" (9:12). This is one of the most important verses concerning Jesus's death, for here he explicitly connects his death to the fulfillment of Scripture. Read in the light of 8:31 and Jesus's statement that the Son of Man "must" suffer, we see that the necessity of Jesus's death is grounded in "God's purposes fulfilled in Scripture."[12] As to which Scriptures Jesus intends, it is tempting to see another reference to Isaiah 53. However, the general nature of Jesus's statement ("it is written") suggests that the Scriptures *as a whole* anticipate Jesus's death.[13]

Jesus's Death Portrayed

Obviously, the death of Jesus comes into sharpest focus in the final section of Mark's Gospel. However, Mark provides more than a chronology of the events leading to Jesus's death. His arrangement of the narrative, his choice of words, and his use of the Scriptures all convey his theological priorities.

As Jesus enters Jerusalem, he receives the adulation of the pilgrims filling the city for the Passover festival (11:8–11). However, when he turns over the tables of the money changers, the Jewish leaders harden their resolve to "destroy him." Nevertheless, fear paralyzes them because of Jesus's hold on the crowds that are "astonished at his teaching" (11:18). This popularity makes them afraid to arrest him (12:12). They decide that the best approach is to trap him. Mark 12 narrates Jesus's conflicts with the Pharisees about paying taxes to Caesar (12:13–17) and with the Sadducees over marriage at the resurrection (12:18–27). These disputes end with a scribe's approval of Jesus's answer to a question about the greatest command (12:28–34). When the scribe affirms

---

12 Schnabel, *Mark*, 198.

13 As Francis Watson, *Paul and the Hermeneutics of Faith* (London: T&T Clark, 2004), 45, suggests, "If attribution to a specific author highlights the text's individuality and distinctiveness, anonymous citation emphasizes its representative character. . . . It is scripture as a whole that speaks these words."

Jesus's response, Jesus tells him, "You are not far from the kingdom of God." After this the leaders are afraid to ask him any more questions (12:34). So much for plan A!

Following Jesus's teaching *in* the temple (12:35–44) and *about* the temple and his coming (13:1–37), the narrative accelerates at the beginning of Mark 14. Mark sets the scene: "two days before the Passover and the Feast of Unleavened Bread" (14:1), signaling that the events will unfold against the backdrop of the Passover and the exodus. Mark further tells us that "the chief priests and the scribes were seeking how to arrest him by stealth and kill him" (14:1). They are, however, still driven by fear, not wanting to arrest him during the festival lest the people revolt (14:2).

Having thus prepared the reader, Mark tells us that a woman anoints Jesus with very expensive perfumed oil at Bethany in the house of Simon the *lepros* (14:3–9). The extravagant waste outrages some, but Jesus understands the significance of the woman's act: she is anointing his body for burial (14:8). This anticipation of Jesus's death is more important than using the money to provide for the poor (14:7). Her costly recognition of Jesus's death will be remembered "wherever the gospel is proclaimed in the whole world" (14:9). Although Mark does not say as much, this prompts Judas's betrayal of Jesus to the chief priests (14:10–11).

The celebration of the Passover (14:12–21) and establishment of the Lord's Supper (14:22–25) follow. Here the scriptural precedents for Jesus's death come into focus. While celebrating the Passover, Jesus speaks of his betrayal and the fact that as the Son of Man he "goes as it is written of him" (14:21). As we saw with 9:12, he again refers to the Scriptures as a whole. However, the next section highlights the Passover in particular. Jesus reinterprets the festival to speak of his own death. The bread represents his body (14:22) and the wine his "blood of the covenant, which is poured out for many" (14:24). These latter words recall the covenantal blood sprinkled by Moses in Exodus 24:8.

Paul understands Jesus's bread-as-body claim to express both Christ's sacrifice and the church as the body of Christ (1 Cor. 10:16–17). Indeed, he goes so far as to cite Jesus's words in 1 Corinthians 11:24–25. Earlier in the same letter he describes Jesus as "our Passover lamb" who "has been sacrificed" (1 Cor. 5:7). We must not miss the redemptive and sacrificial connections that Jesus makes in linking his death with the exodus and the Passover—connections that are picked up by Paul.

When Jesus, with his disciples, goes out to the Mount of Olives, he tells them that all will abandon him and quotes from Zechariah 13:7: "I will strike the shepherd, and the sheep will be scattered" (Mark 14:27). When Peter insists that even if all others fall, he will not, Jesus says that Peter will deny him three times (14:29–30).

Mark 14:32–42 recounts Jesus's prayer to his Father in Gethsemane and the disciples' failure to keep watch with him. This event reveals a very human side of Jesus who is "greatly distressed and troubled" (14:33) and whose soul is "very sorrowful, even to death" (14:34). Jesus prays that "if it were possible, the hour might pass from him" (14:35) and that God would "remove this cup from" him (14:36). He prays this submissively, adding, "Yet not what I will, but what you will" (14:36). Many have gone to their death without this turmoil: none have had to bear the cup of God's wrath. Jesus prays three times—presumably each time asking that he would be spared God's wrath. Finally, the time arrives for the Son of Man to be "betrayed into the hands of sinners" (14:41).

The narrative continues to pick up speed as Jesus's death approaches. While Jesus is speaking with his disciples, Judas appears leading a crowd to arrest him (14:43). Jesus points out the absurdity of it all—coming with clubs and swords when they could easily have seized him while he was teaching in the temple. However, again, he submits to the will of God expressed in Scripture, saying "let the Scriptures be fulfilled" (14:49). Immediately Zechariah 13:7 is fulfilled: all his disciples flee (14:50).

Jesus is tried before the council of the high priest, the chief priests, elders, and scribes who want to condemn him to death (14:53–65). They cannot find any testimony of substance against him (14:55), since the stream of false testimony against him is too contradictory to produce a verdict (14:57–59). However, when the high priest asks Jesus directly if he is "the Christ, the Son of the Blessed," he answers affirmatively and adds that they will "see the Son of Man seated at the right hand of Power, and coming with the clouds of heaven" (14:61–62). The high priest calls this blasphemy, a crime deserving death. They begin to strike and spit at Jesus (14:65). Meanwhile, outside, Peter denies Jesus three times, just as Jesus had predicted.

Also, in line with Jesus's prophecy (10:33), the Jewish leadership hands Jesus over to the Gentiles in the person of Pilate, the Roman governor (15:1–5). When Pilate inquires if he is the "King of the Jews," Jesus simply responds, "You have said so" (15:2). These are Jesus's only words to Pilate, even though the "chief priests accused him of many things" (15:3).

Each Passover Pilate would release a prisoner selected by the crowd (15:6). This year, realizing that the chief priests were acting out of envy (15:10), Pilate offers to release Jesus, "the King of the Jews" (15:9). But the chief priests manipulate the crowd to urge the release of Barabbas— a murderer (15:11). In an ironic reversal of power, Pilate once again appeals to the crowd about Jesus, reminding them that Jesus is an innocent man (15:14). But the crowd clamors all the more that Jesus should be crucified. Pilate relents, releases Barabbas, has Jesus whipped, and consigns him to be crucified.

The injustice is shocking. Pilate scourges and hands over (*paradidōmi*) to crucifixion the innocent one (15:15) while releasing Barabbas, a man "who had committed murder in the insurrection" (15:7). Substituting Jesus for a guilty man fulfills elements of Isaiah 53, for the servant is thereby "numbered with the transgressors" (Isa. 53:12). Mark's verb further solidifies this connection with Isaiah 53:12 (LXX): the servant is handed over (*paradidōmi*) to death. In keeping with the prophecy, salvation for Barabbas means condemnation for Jesus.

Jesus did not die *so that* Barabbas could go free (i.e., in his place). However, by closely associating Jesus's condemnation with Barabbas's release, Mark points in this direction. He narrates the theological truth that Jesus dies in the place of sinners, agreeing not just with Isaiah (Isa. 53:4–6) but with Paul (e.g., Rom. 5:6, 8; 1 Cor. 15:3; 1 Thess. 5:10) and Peter (1 Pet. 3:18). Mark brings us to the very heart of the atonement.

Before crucifying him, Roman soldiers mock Jesus, pretending to honor him as the king of the Jews while hitting and spitting on him (Mark 15:17–20). With few words, Mark describes the moment of crucifixion: "It was the third hour when they crucified him" (15:25). The mocking continues as passersby, the chief priests, and scribes challenge him to come down from the cross. Salvation is at the heart of their taunts: "Save yourself, and come down from the cross. . . . He saved others; he cannot save himself" (15:30–31). They challenge his identity: "Let the Christ, the King of Israel, come down now from the cross that we may see and believe" (15:32). Even the criminals crucified next to him mock Jesus.

Echoing David's words in Psalm 22:1, Jesus cries out, "My God, my God, why have you forsaken me?" (15:34). Confused, the crowd thinks he is calling for Elijah and wonders (perhaps mockingly) if he expects Elijah to come and rescue him. Again using few words, Mark conveys the moment of Jesus's death: "Jesus uttered a loud cry and breathed his last" (15:37).

During the crucifixion, two supernatural events occur. First, darkness comes "over the whole land until the ninth hour" (15:33). Read against an Old Testament background, this appears to be a symbol of God's wrath, darkness being one of the plagues on Egypt (Ex. 10:21–22) and a symbol of eschatological judgment (Amos 8:9). It may also have resonated in a Graeco-Roman context, where the darkness of a solar eclipse could be "associated with the deaths of kings and heroes."[14] Second, at the very moment of Jesus's death, the temple curtain is torn in two (Mark 15:38). This could indicate that Jesus's death brings more direct access to God, but given Jesus's teaching concerning the temple in Mark 13, it more likely prefigures its destruction.

The Roman centurion, upon seeing how Jesus dies, exclaims, "Truly this man was the Son of God!" (15:39). The women we discussed in

---

14   Helen Bond, *The First Biography of Jesus: Genre and Meaning in Mark's Gospel* (Grand Rapids, MI: Eerdmans, 2020), 243.

chapter 5 also watch him die (15:40), thus serving as a model of discipleship by remaining with Jesus to the end.

The final section of Mark 15 describes Jesus's burial. A couple of emphases come through: Joseph of Arimathea, a member of the council who was "looking for the kingdom of God," asks Pilate for the body so that he can bury him in a tomb cut out of rock (15:43, 46). This emphasizes the certainty of Jesus's death, as does the final reference to Pilate who, astonished that Jesus died so quickly, asks the centurion for confirmation before granting the corpse to Joseph (15:45). Thus, Mark provides Jewish (Joseph, Mary, and Mary) and Roman (the centurion) confirmation of Jesus's death.

Jesus's Death and the Old Testament

We have already seen that apart from the Old Testament we cannot understand the significance and meaning of Jesus's death. Many Christians mine the Old Testament for its predictive prophecies concerning Jesus. They seek to establish the *truth* of Jesus's claims about himself by searching the Old Testament for predictions that are realized in his life, and that is certainly legitimate. However, the Old Testament offers more. Even Jesus's most pointed teaching on the purpose of his death—that he "came not to be served but to serve, and to give his life as a ransom for many" (10:45)—cannot be grasped without an understanding of ransom drawn from the Old Testament.

References to Jesus's death appear throughout the Gospel, frequently using categories and expressions drawn from the Old Testament. Perhaps more than any other aspect of his life, Jesus's death and resurrection remind us that to properly understand him we need to read his life against this Old Testament backdrop.

In four places, Jesus directly connects his death with Scripture. Twice he speaks of the Scriptures in general. During the Last Supper Jesus states, "For the Son of Man goes *as it is written* of him, but woe to that man by whom the Son of Man is betrayed!" (14:21). During his arrest in Gethsemane, Jesus states, "Have you come out as against a robber, with swords and clubs to capture me? Day after day I was with you in the temple teaching, and you did not seize me. But *let the Scriptures be fulfilled*" (14:48–49). As Hays notes, the "striking thing about these two declarations is that neither of them specifies any particular *texts* that are to be read as prophecies of the passion."[15] The effect, Hays argues, of not specifying the particular Scriptures is to invite the reader to be alert and to "search carefully" for possible connections between the Scriptures and the events of Jesus's death.[16] A holistic reading of the Old Testament in connection to the death of Jesus is envisioned.

The two marked quotations are Mark 12:10–11 where Psalm 118:22–23 is cited ("have you not read this Scripture") and Mark 14:27 where Zechariah 13:7 is cited ("for it is written"). The fact that these marked quotations are found on the lips of Jesus suggests that the "the central character of the drama provides the explicit hermeneutical clues, while Mark the narrator refrains from overt commentary, subtly weaving scriptural allusions into the fabric of the story."[17]

Jesus cites Psalm 118:22–23 at the end of his parable of the tenants (Mark 12:1–9) to show that Scripture prefigures the Jewish leaders' rejection of him. The leaders grasp that Jesus told this parable against them (12:12). The psalm does two more things. It underlines that, though rejected, Jesus will become the "cornerstone" of a new building. Both Paul (Eph. 2:20) and Peter (1 Pet. 2:6–7) pick up on this, with Peter citing the same psalm as Mark. Jesus will rule a new humanity made up of Jews and Gentiles. Furthermore, the citation stresses the will of God: "This was the Lord's doing" (Mark 12:11). This clearly applies to the rejected stone becoming the cornerstone but also indicates that even the rejection of the stone accorded with the will of God. Mark uses Scripture to highlight that Jesus's death happened by the will of God. He is the one "who is guiding the events of the passion of the Messiah and will bring about his vindication."[18]

---

15   Richard B. Hays, *Echoes of Scripture in the Gospels* (Waco, TX: Baylor University Press, 2016), 79.

16   Hays, *Echoes of Scripture*, 79.

17   Hays, *Echoes of Scripture*, 79.

18   Strauss, *Mark*, 518.

Mark 14:24–28 contains numerous allusions to Zechariah 9–14. Marcus sums them up as follows: my blood of the covenant (Mark 14:24; Zech. 9:11); that day / kingdom of God (Mark 14:25; Zech. 14:4, 9); Mount of Olives (Mark 14:26; Zech. 14:4); strike the shepherd, and sheep will be scattered (Mark 14:27; Zech. 13:7); resurrection / restoration of scattered sheep (Mark 14:28; Zech. 14:4; 13:8–9).[19] The wording of Zechariah 13:7 in Mark 14:27 differs subtly from both the MT and LXX, where God commands an unnamed agent to strike the shepherd. Mark renders it in the first person ("I will strike the shepherd"), emphasizing that God is ultimately responsible for Jesus's death.[20] This accords with Isaiah 53:10: "It was the will of the LORD to crush him." Paul likewise invokes God's sovereignty over Jesus's death when he writes that God "put forward" or "displayed" (*protithēmi*) Christ as a "propitiation" (Rom. 3:25).

Mark also leans on Psalm 22 and its description of the righteous sufferer to portray Jesus's suffering on the cross. He not only presents Jesus quoting Psalm 22:1 at the height of his suffering (Mark 15:34) but also describes the soldiers dividing Jesus's garments and casting lots for them (15:24), echoing Psalm 22:18.[21] However, the question remains, how much of the psalm should we read into Jesus's experience? The psalm speaks of suffering, but it also climaxes with the Lord's deliverance and the fact that despite appearances,

he has not despised or abhorred
the affliction of the afflicted,
and he has not hidden his face from him,
but has heard, when he cried to him. (Ps. 22:24)

19 Joel Marcus, *The Way of the Lord: Christological Exegesis of the Old Testament in the Gospel of Mark* (Louisville: Westminster John Knox, 1992), 157.

20 So, e.g., Adela Yarbro Collins, *Mark: A Commentary on the Gospel of Mark*, Hermeneia (Minneapolis: Fortress, 2007), 670; Strauss, *Mark*, 627.

21 See Rikk E. Watts, "Mark," in *Commentary on the New Testament Use of the Old Testament*, ed. G. K. Beale and D. A. Carson (Grand Rapids, MI: Baker Academic, 2007), 235, for examples of echoes from other "righteous sufferer" psalms—e.g., "betrayal by 'one who eats with me'" (14:18; Ps. 41:9).

It ends in triumph, for all the earth

shall come and proclaim his righteousness to a people yet unborn, that he has done it. (Ps. 22:31)

Commentaries are divided. While we should not be too dogmatic, we can agree with Morna Hooker that "the narrative supplies no evidence to support the contention that Mark had the rest of the psalm in mind."[22] Furthermore, as R. T. France says, "to read into these few tortured words an exegesis of the whole psalm is to turn upside down the effect which Mark has created by this powerful and enigmatic cry of agony."[23] Strauss's observations are worth quoting in full,

> Mark does not provide a theological interpretation of Jesus's words, and we should be cautious about imposing a developed theory of the atonement on them. Still, from the perspective of Markan theology, the best explanation of "why have you forsaken me?" is that Jesus is experiencing the full weight of God's "cup" of judgment (14:36). He is suffering as a ransom payment for the sins of the world (10:45) and pouring out his blood to inaugurate the new covenant (14:24). These ideas of sacrifice, judgment, and ransom are not far from Paul's assertion that "Christ redeemed us from the curse of the law by becoming a curse for us" (Gal 3:13) and that "God made him who had no sin to be sin for us" (2 Cor 5:21).[24]

The Significance of Jesus's Death

Having examined these details concerning Jesus's death, we can step back and consider its overall significance for Mark's theology. Two texts in particular explain the significance of Jesus's death: Mark 10:45 and 14:24.

---

22 Morna D. Hooker, *The Gospel according to Saint Mark*, BNTC (London: Continuum, 1991), 376.

23 R. T. France, *The Gospel of Mark: A Commentary on the Greek Text*, NIGTC (Grand Rapids, MI: Eerdmans, 2002), 652–53.

24 Strauss, *Mark*, 703.

Perhaps the most important commentary on Jesus's death is
10:45 when he teaches the disciples that to be great is to serve one
another. He observes that "even the Son of Man came not to be
served but to serve, and to give his life as a ransom for many." The
phrase "give his life as a ransom for many" is debated. However,
before we turn to consider the meaning and nature of his ransom,
we should observe this incontrovertible and simple point: Jesus
came to die. His death was no secondary consideration. Obviously,
we need to read this in parallel with 1:38 where Jesus says that he
needed to preach throughout Galilee, "for that is why I came." But
Mark stresses Jesus's death, and the question remains, what does
it mean to give his life as a ransom? A ransom to whom? When we
consider the Old Testament background, we see that the ransom
is to the Lord.

There is considerable debate about whether Isaiah 53 lies behind
Jesus's saying. Those who reject this link note that the crucial word
"ransom" (*lytron*), is missing from Isaiah 53. Others argue that while
the term is missing, the theological concepts are present.

The issue might be clarified by considering Exodus 30:11–16 where
a census is taken for the Israelites. Yahweh tells Moses that "each shall
give a ransom for his life to the LORD . . . that there be no plague
among them" (Ex. 30:12). The ransom is a half-shekel, described as
"the LORD's offering to make atonement for your lives" (Ex. 30:15).
The offering thus serves to "propitiate or conciliate God."[25] From this
we see that "ransom" and "propitiation" are "synonymous or closely
related, in some contexts at least."[26] A ransom stays the wrath of
God, just as the servant in Isaiah 53 bears the sins of the people, thus
bringing them peace and healing (Isa. 53:5).

We should further note that throughout the LXX of Isaiah ransom
language is used to describe the Lord, the one who ransoms/redeems
Israel (Isa. 41:14; 43:1, 14; 44:22, 23, 24; 51:11; 52:3; 62:12; 63:9;

25   Adela Yarbro Collins, "Mark's Interpretation of the Death of Jesus," *JBL* 128, no. 3 (2009):
547.
26   Collins, "Mark's Interpretation of the Death of Jesus," 547.

cf. 35:9; 40:2).[27] Isaiah identifies the one who ransoms, the Lord himself, and the means of ransom, the suffering servant. And so, whether or not Isaiah 53 lies behind Mark 10:45, they share the same theological trajectory—God is the one who ransoms his people by the death of his servant. This is confirmed by Paul's use of the related language of redemption using *apolytrōsis*—a cognate of *lytron*. Paul uses this word eschatologically: "we wait eagerly for adoption as sons, the *redemption* of our bodies" (Rom. 8:23). He also uses it soteriologically: Christians "are justified by his grace as a gift, through the *redemption* that is in Christ Jesus" (Rom. 3:24).[28] The context indicates that God accomplishes this redemption through the sacrificial death of Christ (Rom. 3:25).

The other significant explanatory text occurs at the Last Supper when Jesus states, "This is my blood of the covenant, which is poured out for many" (Mark 14:24). The language transports us to Exodus 24:8 where Moses institutes the covenant with the people of Israel and tells them, "Behold the blood of the covenant that the LORD has made with you." Zechariah 9:11 recalls this covenant initiation as God announces his plan to rescue the exiles "because of the blood of my covenant with you."[29] The covenant blood initiates the relationship and is the grounds of God's rescue. These two ideas merge in Jeremiah 31 where the Lord promises a "new covenant" (Jer. 31:31) in which he will "forgive their iniquity, and . . . remember their sin no more" (Jer. 31:34). The "many" for whom Jesus pours out his blood alludes to the "many" rescued by the sin-bearing servant of Isaiah 53:2.

Jesus's Resurrection

In each passion prediction, Jesus states that he will rise again (8:31; 9:31; 10:34). Strikingly, each time he says that this will happen "after three days." The difference between "after three days" and "on the

---

27 Ben Witherington, III, *The Gospel of Mark: A Socio-Rhetorical Commentary* (Grand Rapids, MI: Eerdmans, 2001), 288–90.

28 Michael P. Theophilus, "The Roman Connection: Paul and Mark," in *Paul and Mark: Comparative Essays Part I: Two Authors at the Beginnings of Christianity*, ed. Oda Wischmeyer, David C. Sim, and Ian J. Elmer, BZNW 198 (Berlin: De Gruyter, 2014), 63.

29 Schnabel, *Mark*, 357.

third day"—the more common expression in the rest of the New Testament[30]—is not significant, but the consistent reference to "three" /
"third" across the New Testament is.

Luke (24:46) and Paul (1 Cor. 15:4) both understand that the reference to Jesus rising on the third day derives from Scripture. Although
Mark does not specifically tie the three-day period to the Old Testament, the frequency with which he repeats it suggests it has a similar
importance for him. And given his allusive manner of referring to the
Scriptures, it is likely that they account for the presence of the reference.
The most common suggestion for a scriptural background is Hosea 6:2:

> After two days he will revive us;
>> on the third day he will raise us up,
>> that we may live before him.

The objection that Hosea envisages the resurrection of the nation "is
precisely to miss the point of Jesus's identification in his person of the
Son of Man . . . with Israel."[31]

The reference to three days reappears at Jesus's trial before the council
where false witnesses testify that he would destroy the temple and "in
three days" build another (Mark 14:58). This charge is repeated when
the crowd mocks him on the cross (15:29).

Before reaching his resurrection narrative in 16:1–8, Mark foreshadows the event. In 14:25 Jesus speaks of drinking "of the fruit of
the vine" in "that day when I drink it new in the kingdom of God."
In 14:28 Jesus tells the disciples, "after I am raised up, I will go before you to Galilee." The conclusion to the parable of the tenants
also hints at the resurrection when Jesus cites Psalm 118:22–23 in
Mark 12:10–11: "the stone that the builders rejected has become the
cornerstone." The rejected Son of Man will become the cornerstone
through the resurrection.

---

30 Cf. Matt. 16:21; 17:23; 20:19; 27:64; Luke 9:22;13:32; 18:33; 24:7, 21, 46; Acts 10:40; 1 Cor.
    15:4. Matthew has both in 27:63–64. See Strauss, *Mark*, 364.
31 Watts, "Mark," 177.

The actual narrative of the resurrection is briefer than the other Gospels (if we take the short ending of Mark as original). Jesus himself does not appear. Instead, the women who go to his tomb find a man—presumably an angel—who tells them that Jesus "has risen; he is not here" (16:6). He points to the place where they laid Jesus as evidence that Jesus is gone and tells the women to go to Galilee where "you will see him, just as he told you" (16:7).

Why such a brief account of the aftermath of the resurrection? The longer endings of Mark point to an early perceived lack in the Gospel, with scribes providing what they thought Mark's account lacked. But if we read this book as "the beginning of the gospel," the lack of a long resurrection narrative is to be expected. Mark ends at precisely the point that early preaching (at least judged by the book of Acts) began—the resurrection of Christ. The seeming anticlimax of the women fleeing in silence and fear may relate to "the situation of [Mark's] primary recipients, who were either experiencing or fearful of persecution."[32]

In addition, as Margaret Mitchell argues, Mark shares with Paul what she calls *synecdochical hermeneutics*. By this she means that "every time one episode of the foundational narrative is named, the others are thereby assumed and incorporated."[33] Put simply, she argues that for Mark as for Paul when the death of Christ is mentioned, the resurrection is assumed. This connection between Jesus's death and resurrection makes the gospel the gospel. Furthermore, their connection has already been established by the three passion predictions—in each the death of Christ is followed by the resurrection. Even apart from these arguments and without a narration of appearances by the risen Christ, Mark clearly indicates that Christ has been raised: the young man testifies, "He has risen; he is not here" (16:6).

---

32 Bond, *First Biography*, 252.

33 Margaret Mitchell, "Mark, the Long-Form Pauline εὐαγγέλιον," in *Modern and Ancient Literary Criticism of the Gospels: Continuing the Debate on Gospel Genre(s)*, ed. R. M. Calhoun, D. P. Moessner, and T. Nicklas, WUNT 451 (Tübingen: Mohr Siebeck, 2020), 213.

Mark 16:6–7 parallels 1 Corinthians 15:3b–5. Although the order differs (the text of Mark 16:6–7 is rearranged in the table below), the episodes are the same:[34]

Comparison of 1 Cor. 15:3b–5 and Mark 16:6–7

1 Cor. 15:3b–5	Mark 16:6–7
Christ died	Jesus of Nazareth, who was crucified
he was buried,	See the place where they laid him
he was raised	He has risen
he appeared	you will see him,
to Cephas, then to the twelve	his disciples and Peter

Luke alone of the Gospel writers narrates Jesus's ascension. It is nevertheless alluded to in Mark's Gospel. When the disciples object to the waste of the jar of perfumed oil, which could have been sold and the money given to the poor, Jesus replies that although the poor will always be with them, "you will not always have me" (Mark 14:7). By itself this may be ambiguous, but Jesus has already cited Psalm 110:1 with its reference to sitting at God's right hand in Mark 12:36. Moreover, the return of the Son of Man in glory in 13:26 also points to his post-resurrection ascension, as does his absence presupposed in 13:21.

Conclusion

Although Mark wrote more than a "passion narrative with an extended introduction," the death of Jesus is his most significant theme. Pulling together our observations allows us to summarize the significance of this death.

First, Jesus's death brings atonement. If we read 10:45 and 14:24 in light of Old Testament ransom language, then sacrificial and atoning ideas become prominent. Jesus's teaching that his blood is the "blood

---

34 Gerd Theissen, "'Evangelium' im Markusevangelium," in *Modern and Ancient Literary Criticism of the Gospels: Continuing the Debate on Gospel Genre(s)*, ed. R. M. Calhoun, D. P. Moessner, and T. Nicklas, WUNT 451 (Tübingen: Mohr Siebeck, 2020), 78. I have rendered Theissen's German by lightly adjusting the ESV.

of the covenant, which is poured out for many" both solidifies the atoning significance of his death and ties it back to the Old Testament.

Second, Jesus's death serves as a model for disciples to imitate. He says as much in 8:34—to be a disciple means taking up one's cross and following him. The imitation motif also finds its negative counterpoint as his disciples fail at Gethsemane, flee, and even deny him.[35]

Third, Jesus's death points to both poles of his identity: he is both King and servant. His crucifixion expresses his servant nature. Jesus willingly dies as an innocent man for the sins of others, expressing his status as "slave of all" (10:44).[36] Like "the good philosopher, Jesus has a fitting death, an extension of his earlier way of life."[37] But his death also underlines his identity as God's King. Nobody calls him "King" until "he stands before Pilate on the way to the cross; yet from that point forward, within the space of thirty verses, he is called 'king' six times: three times by Pilate (15:2, 9,12), twice by mockers just before and just after his crucifixion (15:18, 32), and once by the inscription over his cross (15:26)."[38] Indicators of Jesus's kingship increase along with markers of his passivity. From his bold speech before the high priest (14:62), to two words before Pilate (15:2), he remains silent until his cry on the cross.[39]

At the beginning of the chapter, I asked whether Mark says more than Paul's statement in 1 Corinthians 15:3 that "Christ died for our sins." This can be answered by considering another verse from Paul's letters. He reminds the Galatians that in his preaching "Jesus Christ was publicly portrayed as crucified" before "your eyes" (Gal. 3:1). Mark's narrative accomplishes what Paul was doing in his preaching. As we read, we have access into the very "heart" of the gospel.[40]

---

35 Bond, *First Biography*, 235.
36 Bond, *First Biography*, 233.
37 Bond, *First Biography*, 250.
38 Joel Marcus, "Crucifixion as Parodic Exaltation," *JBL* 125, no. 1 (2006): 73.
39 Bond, *First Biography*, 227.
40 Mitchell, "Mark, the Long-Form Pauline εὐαγγέλιον," 213.

Epilogue

The End of the Beginning

WHAT IS MARK'S GOSPEL? This simple question has kept bread on the table for scholars for many years. The consensus has shifted from seeing the Gospels as a form of unique Christian literature to classifying them as examples of ancient biographies, albeit with some unique features. Reading Mark in this way creates an expectation of a life of Jesus written to call for imitation. This approach fits much of what we have seen in Mark—particularly the emphasis on discipleship—but cannot capture everything in the Gospel.

Jesus's life offers more than a pattern to be imitated; it is part of a greater, theological reality. We have seen at many points that his life fulfills the Old Testament. His arrival inaugurates the kingdom of God. His death in particular *had* to happen to fulfill the Scriptures. But his life, teaching, and death also are the foundation of the gospel. Jesus anticipated aspects of his life, such as his anointing by the woman at Bethany (14:3–9), becoming part of the proclamation of the gospel.

Mark, in giving us "the beginning of the gospel," has made the historical and theological connection between Jesus's life and apostolic preaching, preeminently that of Paul. Paul reflects on his ministry in a number of places, perhaps none in such a profoundly Christological way as 2 Corinthians 4:1–12. Gospel ministry in its simplicity merely provides an "open statement of the truth" (2 Cor. 4:2) whereby the apostles proclaim "not ourselves, but Jesus Christ as Lord" (2 Cor. 4:5).

Its profundity is seen in the fact that the apostles always carry "in the body the death of Jesus, so that the life of Jesus may also be manifested in [their] bodies" (2 Cor. 4:10). Their experience of being "given over to death for Jesus' sake" was "so that the life of Jesus also may be manifested in [their] mortal flesh" (2 Cor. 4:11). In Galatians Paul stresses that he bears on his body "the marks of Jesus" (Gal. 6:17) and reminds his recipients that in his preaching "Jesus Christ was publicly portrayed as crucified" before their eyes (Gal. 3:1)

For Paul, gospel preaching was a way of "manifesting the life of Jesus." He "regarded himself as a one-man multi-media parade of Jesus Christ crucified (and risen)."[1] The Gospel of Mark in an analogous way powerfully manifests the life of Jesus. It puts its readers in the privileged position of those who approached Jesus and received "the secret of the kingdom" (Mark 4:11).

In narrating the beginning of the gospel, Mark enables this same encounter with Jesus in narrative form. The words of Jesus call Mark's readers to the same Christ-revealing life that Paul lived: "If anyone would come after me, let him deny himself and take up his cross and follow me" (8:34).

As we read Mark and encounter Jesus, we are called to follow him and gain comfort from his death as a ransom (10:45), which makes the impossible possible: the salvation of human beings (10:27). The open-ended nature of Mark invites its readers to follow the Lord Jesus and lose their lives for his and the gospel's sake (8:35).

This book is about Mark's Gospel and is therefore a book about Jesus. But in it I have tried to show that Mark's portrayal of Jesus, while complete and coherent on its own terms, is best read in conversation with Peter and Paul. Mark narrates "the beginning of the gospel" that was already being preached by Peter and Paul. Mark represents something of a bridge between these two great apostles—one the apostle to the circumcised and the other to the uncircumcised. At the end of Peter's second letter, he reflects on this relationship. While he acknowledges

---

1   Margaret Mitchell, "Mark, the Long-Form Pauline εὐαγγέλιον," in *Modern and Ancient Literary Criticism of the Gospels: Continuing the Debate on Gospel Genre(s)*, ed. R. M. Calhoun, D. P. Moessner, and T. Nicklas, WUNT 451 (Tübingen: Mohr Siebeck, 2020), 209.

that Paul writes some things that are "hard to understand," nevertheless his letters have the same authority as the "other Scriptures" (2 Pet. 3:16). He then concludes with an exhortation that Paul would endorse and that can be fulfilled as we read Mark's Gospel: "Grow in the grace and knowledge of our Lord and Savior Jesus Christ. To him be the glory both now and to the day of eternity. Amen" (2 Pet. 3:18).

Recommended Resources

Commentaries

Edwards, James R. *The Gospel according to Mark*. PNTC. Grand Rapids, MI: Eerdmans, 2002.

France, R. T. *The Gospel of Mark: A Commentary on the Greek Text*. NIGTC. Grand Rapids, MI: Eerdmans, 2002.

Schnabel, Eckhard J. *Mark: An Introduction and Commentary*. TNTC. Downers Grove, IL: IVP Academic, 2017.

Stein, Robert H. *Mark*. BECNT. Grand Rapids, MI: Baker Academic, 2008.

Strauss, Mark L. *Mark*. ZECNT. Grand Rapids, MI: Zondervan Academic, 2014.

Monographs

Aernie, Jeffrey W. *Narrative Discipleship: Patterns of Women in the Gospel of Mark*. Eugene, OR: Pickwick, 2018.

Bauckham, Richard. *Jesus and the Eyewitnesses: The Gospels as Eyewitness Testimony*. 2nd ed. Grand Rapids, MI: Eerdmans, 2017.

Bird, Michael F. *Jesus is the Christ: The Messianic Testimony of the Gospels*. Downers Grove, IL: IVP Academic, 2012.

Garland, David E. *A Theology of Mark's Gospel: Good News about Jesus the Messiah, the Son of God*. Biblical Theology of the New Testament. Grand Rapids, MI: Zondervan Academic, 2015.

Gathercole, Simon. *The Preexistent Son: Recovering the Christologies of Matthew, Mark, and Luke*. Grand Rapids, MI: Eerdmans, 2006.

Hays, Richard B. *Echoes of Scripture in the Gospels*. Waco, TX: Baylor University Press, 2016.

Articles

Bird, Michael F. "Mark: Interpreter of Peter and Disciple of Paul." Pages 30–61 in *Paul and the Gospels: Christologies, Conflicts and Convergences*. Edited by Michael F. Bird and Joel Willits. LNTS 411. London: T&T Clark, 2011.

Watts, Rikk E. "Mark." Pages 111–249 in *Commentary on the New Testament Use of the Old Testament*. Edited by G. K. Beale and D. A. Carson. Grand Rapids, MI: Baker Academic, 2007.

General Index

Scripture Index

New Testament Theology

Edited by Thomas R. Schreiner and Brian S. Rosner, this series presents clear, scholarly overviews of the main theological themes of each book of the New Testament, examining what they reveal about God and his relation to the world in the context of the overarching biblical narrative.

For more information, visit **crossway.org**.